MW00532572

I will drink from your fountain, and so live.

AUGUSTINE
(354–430)

FOUNT OF HEAVEN

PRAYERS
of the
EARLY CHURCH

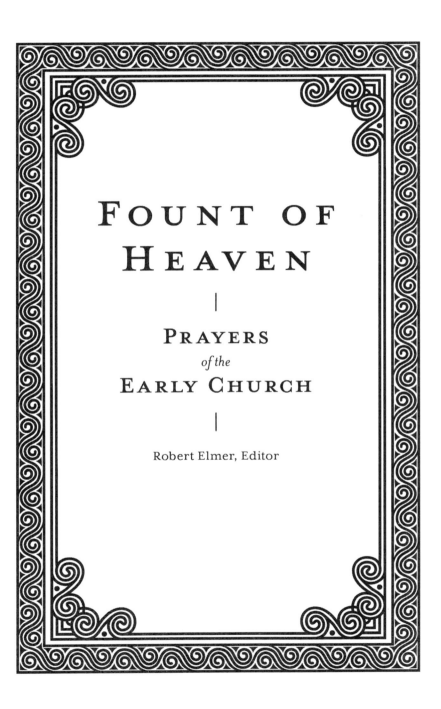

FOUNT OF HEAVEN

|

PRAYERS
of the
EARLY CHURCH

|

Robert Elmer, Editor

Fount of Heaven: Prayers of the Early Church

Copyright 2022 Robert Elmer

Lexham Press, 1313 Commercial St., Bellingham, WA 98225
LexhamPress.com

Print ISBN 9781683596288
Digital ISBN 9781683596295
Library of Congress Control Number 9781683596288

Lexham Editorial: Elliot Ritzema, Kelsey Matthews, Abigail Stocker, Danielle Thevenaz
Cover Design: Brittany Schrock
Typesetting: Justin Marr

SEND US PEACE, GRACE, AND HEALING

Open the sea of love to us · Pour out your promise to us, Lord · Show us your rainbow, Lord · Make us happy in you · How you have loved us! · You are able to provide · Your power subdues all · Work for me your resurrection · Heal those who are sick, Lord · Receive us into your presence, Lord · Show us your majesty · You provide our endless home · Whisper peace · Keep us, the descendants of Adam and Eve · Redeem me from that old life · Hear me in your grace · Help us flee from vice · Bring us rain, Lord

PROTECT US, LORD

For help in the midst of persecution · Help me, you who need nothing · Show us the way onward · The war being waged against us · Keep me until that day, Lord · You are the garland on my head

HELP US TO BE MORE LIKE JESUS

Be gracious to us · Help us love one another · We will keep knocking on your door · Clothe us with fire, Lord · Stretch your wings over us · Help us to leave behind our worries · We pray from Genesis to Revelation · Restrain our thoughts · For gifts like stars · Let me always seek your face · Give me a pure heart · We will love you with our whole heart · Help us to shine and rest with you · Help us find humility

LET US KNOW JESUS BETTER

Let me see your face · I will grow into you, Lord · Help me to find real life · Kindle us and draw us close · Now my soul is free · I love you above all else · I heard your voice behind me · You are the source · Teach me to come closer to you · Convert me wholly to you

INTRODUCTION

Scripture tells us in Luke 11:1 that the original twelve disciples asked Jesus how to pray. It was a good question then, and one worth asking again today.

To help answer that question, this collection of prayers seeks to open a window into the souls of the first generations of believers—real people whose hearts beat with praise in the face of trouble and persecution. As we share in their prayers, we discover new depth for our own. So let's consider for a moment the world in which these early believers found themselves.

The turbulent centuries immediately following Christ's earthly ministry might seem an unlikely time for new faith to flourish. But it did. Despite the danger of persecution and death, people of the Way spread out across the Roman world and eagerly shared what they believed. Home churches and prayer meetings flourished even as the mighty empire crumbled. And by the early 300s, Christians could be found virtually everywhere around the Mediterranean— from Syria to Greece, Italy to North Africa and Egypt, Turkey and beyond.

It was as if a nuclear bomb of faith had detonated, with Jerusalem as its epicenter. In wave after wave, Christian communities grew to include men and women from all levels of society, slave and aristocrat alike.

As the church grew, its worship services, sermons, instructions, and prayers found their way into writing, carefully recorded by people with names like Clement and Polycarp, Ambrose and Augustine. Many of these early Christian leaders had turned from wealth and status to embrace the new faith.

It would be a costly choice in more ways than one. During periods of persecution, some paid with their lives when they refused to take the easy path of accommodation and survival by bowing before the altars of Roman emperor worship. Still, they prayed together with an awe and reverence that recognized God's power, preeminence, and holiness. They wrote about their faith with an effusive, mystery-filled joy that is rare today.

As these early Christians waded through deep waters, personal issues seemed to take a back seat to the all-consuming glory of their three-in-one God. Their outward-focused prayers are typically all about "thee," not "me." They seemed to have little time for the luxury of self-centered drama.

So what could have motivated those people to cling so stubbornly to a highly dangerous faith? And what would they have wanted us to know? The answers to such questions, if taken seriously, could have a profound effect on our faith today.

We find in the words of their prayers that their understanding of God mattered a great deal. These believers wrestled with theology, argued theology, wrote mountains of books (by hand!) about theology, and held conferences about theology.

In other words, truth mattered. Doctrine mattered. Details and shades of meaning—it all mattered. And in their search for truth, eventually those Christians hammered and molded what they believed into creeds that are still recited today by their spiritual heirs.

Our world still desperately needs the truth for which those believers lived and died because the serpent still whispers, "Did God really say...?" In response, Irenaeus of Lyons once prayed about his own writing for God to "help every reader of this book to know you, that you are God alone, and to be strengthened in you, and to avoid every heretical, godless, and irreverent doctrine."[1]

Heretical, godless, and irreverent? By current standards, these terms seem prickly and intolerant. Yet they stand as useful markers to help us navigate past the deadly shoals of shallow belief and unexamined faith.

We face many of the same challenges as the early Christians—among them, the unending challenge to maintain a more vibrant and consistent prayer life. As the noted theologian and church leader Jerome wrote in the early fifth century,

> *I stand to pray; I could not pray, if I did not believe; but if I really believed, I should cleanse that heart of mine with which God is seen, I should beat my hands upon my breast, the tears would stream down my cheeks, my body would shudder, my face grow pale, I should lie at my Lord's feet, weep over them, and wipe them with my hair, I should cling to the cross and not let go my hold until I obtained mercy. But, as it is, frequently in my prayers I am either walking in the arcades, or calculating my interest, or am carried away with base thoughts, so as to be occupied with things the mere mention of which*

*makes me blush. Where is our faith? Are we to suppose
that it was thus that Jonah prayed? Or the three youths?
Or Daniel in the lion's den? Or the robber on the cross?*²

Jerome recognized his own weaknesses, and perhaps they
mirror our own. Yet he and his contemporaries also had
the long game in mind—their impact on future generations.
This collection seeks to build a bridge between those early
prayers and us, spanning the centuries to enrich and inspire
renewed daily prayer.

This bridge brings us into closer contact with the hearts and
pens of Christ-followers who enjoyed precious few degrees
of separation from events recorded in the Gospels. Several
of the earliest writers may even have had direct contact
with an original apostle (John or Peter, for example).

Not every writer was a professional theologian, priest, or
church leader, however. A few, like Ausonius, were simply
early believers who happened to leave behind a personal
account that survived the centuries. Typically, the writings
were then translated from the original Latin, Greek, or
Syriac sometime in the nineteenth century. I've edited
and abridged the antiquated English wording for clarity,
updating the text for today's reader. In some cases, early
sermons have been modified through light edits. In others,
early prayers flowed organically from the middle of a
homily or apologetic message.

Note also that the authorship of individual writings may
occasionally be disputed or in question—but that is to
be expected for writings of this vintage. To be clear, the
purpose of this book is not to authenticate or disprove

scholarly claims that have seesawed between divergent conclusions over the years. That is beyond our scope. For example, did Clement of Rome actually pen all the prayers ascribed to him in the *Apostolic Constitutions*? Scholars may disagree. Or who wrote the *Didache*? We're not sure.

Yet I am convinced the original authors would have been pleased to have us borrow their words for our own prayers. After all, these are not just a window into the distant past, but a reminder of First Things. In these prayers are recorded *what really matters.* And if it were possible, we would thank our earliest brothers and sisters for the way they held firmly to faith, and to our Savior, even on the worst of days.

Perhaps we can know a measure of this same dedication as we pray once more the prayers they prayed.

—*Robert Elmer*

LIST OF AUTHORS

ADÆUS AND MARIS (c. 200)

AMBROSE OF MILAN (340–397)

ANATOLIUS OF CONSTANTINOPLE (died 458)

APOSTOLIC CONSTITUTIONS (c. 380)

ARNOBIUS (died 330)

ATHENOGENES (died 305)

AUGUSTINE OF HIPPO (354–430)

AUSONIUS (310–395)

BASIL OF CAESAREA (330–379)

JOHN CASSIAN (360–430)

JOHN CHRYSOSTOM (345–407)

CLEMENT OF ALEXANDRIA (150–215)

CLEMENT OF ROME (35–101)

CYRIL OF JERUSALEM (315–386)

THE DIDACHE (first century)

EPHRAIM THE SYRIAN (306–373)

EUSEBIUS (260–340)

GREGORY NAZIANZEN (325–389)

GREGORY OF NYSSA (335–395)

HILARY OF POITIERS (300–367)

IRENAEUS OF LYONS (130–200)

LACTANTIUS (230–325)

MELITO OF SARDIS (died 180)

METHODIUS OF OLYMPIA (died 311)

ODES OF SOLOMON (c. 125)

PAULINUS PELLAEUS (377–461)

POLYCARP (69–155)

PSEUDO-MACARIUS

SERAPION SCHOLASTICUS (died 370)

SHAMUNA THE MARTYR (died 293)

SYNESIUS (375–413)

TERTULLIAN (155–220)

THEODORET (393–458)

VENANTIUS (530–609)

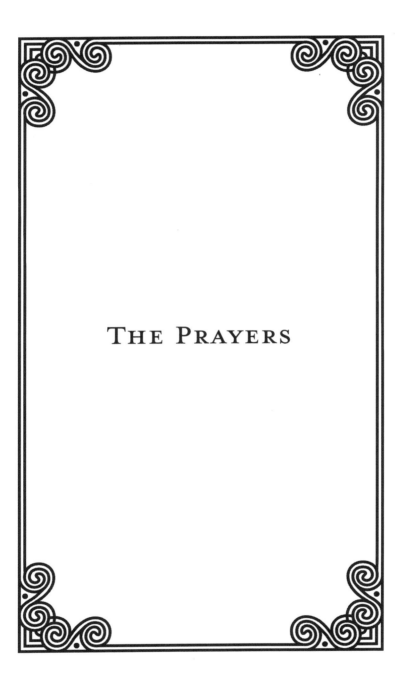

THE PRAYERS

HELP US TO PRAISE

WHOEVER SEEKS WILL PRAISE

Great are you, O Lord, and greatly to be praised.

Great is your power. Your wisdom is infinite, and we praise you.

We, who are just a particle of your creation. We, who carry our mortality with us—the witness of our sin, and the witness that you resist the proud.

Yet we praise you.

You awaken us to delight in your praise. For you made us for yourself, and our heart is restless until it finds its place of rest in you.

Grant me, Lord, to know and understand which is first: to call on you, or to praise you? To know you, or to call on you? For who can call on you, not knowing you? Whoever does not know you might call on you as someone other than you really are.

Or rather, do we call on you so that we may know you? But how do they call on him in whom they have not believed? Or how will they believe without a preacher? (Romans 10:14).

And whoever seeks the Lord will praise him: for they that seek will find him, and they that find will praise him.

I will seek you, Lord, by calling on you. And I will call on you, believing in you, because you have been preached to us.

With the faith you have given me, I will call on you. That faith has inspired me, through the incarnation of your Son, through the ministry of the preacher.

Amen.

— *Augustine of Hippo*

We set our hope on your name

Help us to set our hope on your name, Lord. You are the origin and source of all creation. You open the eyes of our hearts so we can know you.

You alone abide highest in the lofty place. You are holy in the holy. You lay low the insolence of the proud, set the lowly on high, and bring down the lofty. You make rich and poor, give life and death. You alone are the benefactor of spirits and the God of all flesh.

You look into the deepest places and see all our works. You help and relieve those who are in peril, and you are the savior of those in despair. You are the creator and overseer of every spirit.

You multiply the nations and have chosen out all who love you through Jesus Christ, your beloved Son, through whom you taught us, honored us, and set us apart.

Amen.

— *Clement of Rome*

This prayer is widely regarded as the earliest recorded Christian prayer outside of Scripture.

WE PRAY TO STIR UP DEVOTION

Lord, since eternity is yours, do you not know of what I
speak to you? Or do you see in time, what passes in time?
Why then do I so often speak to you in time?

Truly I do not pray so you will learn from me, but to stir up
my devotion toward you. We pray so that we all may say,
"Great is the Lord, and greatly to be praised."

I have said it already, and will say it again: I do this for
the love of your love.

For we pray also, and yet Truth (that is, Jesus himself) has
said, "Your Father knows what you need before you ask him"
(Matthew 6:8).

So it is our affections that we lay open to you, confessing our
own miseries, and your mercies on us.

Through prayer, you may free us wholly. Through prayer, we
may cease to be miserable in ourselves, and blessed in you.

Through prayer, we see how you have called us to become
poor in spirit, and meek, and mourners, hungering and
thirsting after righteousness.

Through prayer, we learn to become merciful, and pure in
heart, and peacemakers.

See, I have told you many things, as I could and as I would,
because you first wanted me to confess unto you, my Lord God.
For you are good, and your mercy endures forever, amen.

— *Augustine of Hippo*

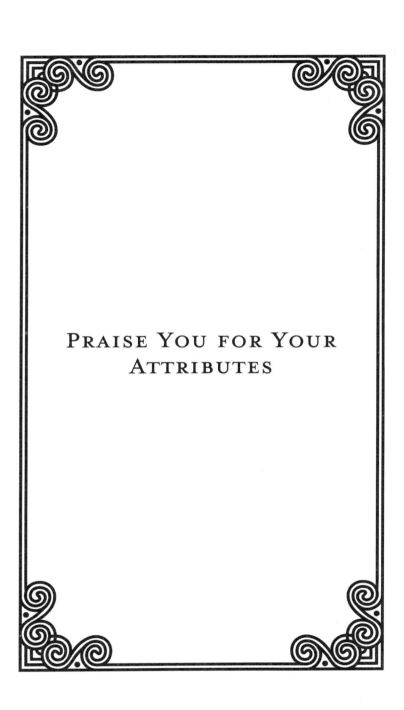

Praise You for Your Attributes

To the Lord, the true life

I pray to you, O Lord, the highest truth. You are the one through whom is true all that is true.

I pray to you, O Lord, the true life. You are the one through whom all things live that do live.

You are the highest blessing, and through you are blessed all that are blessed.

You are the highest good and beauty, and the light through which we can know and understand.

I pray to you, Lord who has the whole world in your hands, although we cannot see, smell, hear, taste, or touch you. But we take all the good laws and virtues that we have from your realm. From your realm we have examples for all the good we can do.

Everyone who flees from you falls, everyone who turns to you rises, and everyone who abides in you stands. No wise person forsakes you, only the wise seek you, and no one completely finds you except the pure in heart.

Those who forsake you perish. Those who love you, seek you. And those who follow you, have you.

The truths you gave us awaken us from the sleep of our sins, and the love you have given us binds us to you. Our hope lifts us to you. Through you we overcome our enemies, both spiritual and in this world.

You who forgive, draw near and have mercy on me,
because you have given us a great gift: We will never
perish and come to nothing.

Amen.

— Augustine of Hippo

YOUR WORD IS LIKE A MIRROR

Those who are not Jews now praise you because your
word has become like a mirror—and in that mirror we
could see death, secretly swallowing up our lives.

For those of us who used to chase gods who were no gods,
you who were God came after us. And by your words, like
a bridle in a horse's mouth, you turned us from the many
gods to the one true God, the Mighty One.

You drew us to the cross.

To you be glory who has taken away that false religion that
caused us to stumble. Medicine of life, to you be praise—
you who have converted all who are baptized.

Praise be to you who are the life of all, and the Lord of all!
The lost who are found bless you, and you have given joy
to the angels.

Amen.

— Ephraim the Syrian

GREAT PROTECTOR, YOU ARE BLESSED FOREVER

Great protector of Abraham's descendants, you are blessed forever.

Starting from the truth which our forefather knew when he changed his way, you guided him by a vision, and you taught him about this world. What you taught him went before his faith, his faith grew from what you taught him, and the covenant grew out of his faith.

For you said: "I will make your offspring like the dust of the earth, so that if anyone could count the dust, then your offspring could be counted" (Genesis 13:16 NIV).

You gave him Isaac, and you were called his God, saying, "I will be with you and will bless you. For to you and your descendants I will give all these lands and will confirm the oath I swore to your father Abraham" (Genesis 26:3).

When our father Jacob was sent into Mesopotamia, you said to him, "I am going to make you fruitful and increase your numbers. I will make you a community of peoples, and I will give this land as an everlasting possession to your descendants after you" (Genesis 48:4).

And so you spoke also to Moses, your faithful and holy servant, at the vision of the bush, when you said, "I AM WHO I AM. This is my name forever, the name you shall call me from generation to generation" (Exodus 3:14–15).

Great protector of Abraham's descendants, you are blessed forever, amen.

— Apostolic Constitutions

WHO DO I LOVE WHEN I LOVE YOU, LORD?

I love you, Lord, with knowing and assurance—not with doubt. You struck my heart with your word, and I loved you.

Heaven and earth, and all that is within them, they urge me to love you. They never stop saying the same to everyone, so no one has an excuse.

But you will have deeper mercy on whom you will have mercy, and you will have compassion for whom you have compassion. Otherwise, heaven and earth speak praises to deaf ears.

But what do I love when I love you? Not a beautiful physical body, or the fair harmony of time. Not the brightness of light, so good to our eyes. Not the sweet melodies of song, and not the fragrant smell of flowers and spices, and not manna or honey. Not the embrace of a warm hug.

I love none of these when I love you, Lord. Yet I love a kind of light, and a kind of melody. I love a kind of fragrance, and meat, and embrace, when I love you.

It is the light, melody, fragrance, meat, and embrace of my inner self, where shines into my soul what space cannot contain. It sounds in a way that time cannot erase. The fragrance and the taste never fade, and the embrace clings forever.

That is what I love when I love you, God.

Amen.

— Augustine of Hippo

PRAISE FOR THE INDESCRIBABLE

O greatest, Supreme Creator of things invisible! You who are yourself unseen, and who cannot be comprehended! You are worthy, you are so worthy—if only we mortals may speak of you.

All who breathe and think should never cease to feel thankful and to give you thanks. Through our entire lives we should fall on our knees before you and offer never-ending prayers.

For you are the first cause, and in you all created things exist. You are the foundation for all things.

You are limitless, unbegotten, immortal, enduring forever. You are God yourself alone, uncontainable, of virtues indescribable, of greatness indefinable.

You cannot be held to a single place; your movement cannot be restricted. Our words cannot define you.

To understand you, we must be silent. Our attempts would only track you through a shady cloud.

Grant a pardon, King Supreme, to those who would persecute your servants.

We are not surprised if you are beyond knowing. We are more astonished if you were clearly comprehended.

Amen.

— *Arnobius*

You give life to the lifeless

Almighty One, I know you through the worship of my heart alone. To the wicked you are unknown, yet you are known to every soul who is devoted to you.

You are without beginning and without end, more ancient than time past and time to come. No mind can grasp, nor tongue express, your being and extent.

The only one who may behold you and, face to face, hear your commands and sit at your fatherly right hand is himself the maker of all things. He himself is the cause of all created things. He himself is the Word of God, the Word which is God, who was before the world which he was to make, begotten at that time when time was not yet, who came into being before the sun's beams and the bright morning star lit up the sky.

Nothing was made without him, and through him all things were made. His throne is in heaven, and beneath his seat lie earth and the sea and the invincible chaos of dark night. Unresting, he is the mover of all things, the one who gives life to the lifeless.

He is God, the begotten of the unbegotten.

Stirred to action by the betrayal of those people who scorned him, he called the nations into his kingdom to worship him, as worthier offshoots of an ingrafted stock.

To our forefathers it was granted to behold him, and whoever recognized him as God saw the Father also.

He bore our sinful stains and suffered death with mockery.
He taught us that there is a road leading back to eternal
life, and that the soul returns not alone, but with the body
complete enters the realms of heaven and leaves the secret
chamber of the grave empty, covered with earth which
cannot hold it.

Amen.

— *Ausonius*

IN YOU WE ARE COMPLETE

I call on you, God. You are the truth—and all things are
true in you, from you, and through you.

You are the wisdom—and all things are wise in you, from
you, and through you.

You are the true and crowning life—and all things live in
you, from you, and through you.

You are the blessedness—and all things are blessed in you,
from you, and through you.

You are the good—and all things are good in you, from
you, and through you.

To be turned away from you, God, is to fall—but to be
turned back is to rise again. And to abide in you is to stand
firm. To go forth from you, Lord, is to die—but returning
to you is revival. To have a dwelling in you is life.

No one loses you, unless deceived. No one seeks you, unless stirred up. No one finds you, unless made pure. To forsake you is to perish.

Faith rouses us toward you, God. Hope lifts us up, and love joins us together. Through you, we overcome the enemy, and you are the one we come to with our requests. It is your gift that we do not utterly perish.

Through you, Lord, we flee evil and follow the good. Through you, we do not give up in the face of disaster. And through you, the baits and enticements of evil have no power to hold us.

In you, Lord, we are complete—even with fewer possessions. You strip us of that which is not, and array us in those things that truly are. Death is swallowed up in victory, and you turn us to yourself. You make us worthy to be heard, you fortify us, and you lead us into all truth.

Lord, you only speak good to us, and you call us back into the way. You lead us to the door of life, and open it when we knock.

You give us the bread of life. Through you we thirst for a drink, and when we drink, we never thirst again.

You convince the world of sin, righteousness, and judgment—and through you, we are freed from bondage. You cleanse us and prepare us for rewards in heaven.

Come to me in your mercy!

Amen.

— Augustine of Hippo

COME, FOUNTAIN OF LIGHT

True Son of the eternal King, before the foundations of the earth were laid.

Lord, Father of all, by which was born the Christ. A virgin's pain brought the Light of Life to a forlorn world. A man! And yet, of ages gone—and of all ages yet to come. Throughout eternity, you are the one, the upholder, the perfecter, and the sun.

You are the fountain of light, O Christ, and light of the Father's light. You are the bright ray. You swept away the darkness, turning night to day.

You are the founder of the world, who molded the starry sphere. The moon borrows its power from you, easing the gloom of night.

Through you, the year is crowned with its fruit. Flocks and herds are fed. You make the ground bring forth with its harvest. You give bread to the poor.

From your overflowing supply of indescribable grace and love, you pour fertile sunshine over the surface of every world. From you spring forth light, mind, and soul.

Fountain of love, we bless you, Father, our rock and strength. Divine Son, and Holy Breath, who crowns you both.

Spirit, your gifts bring us to life as they roll over us like waves.

You with the Father, send him down to cheer and fertilize my soul.

Amen.

— Synesius

WHAT DO WE CALL YOU?

Supreme One, who is over all, what other name can we call you, in your greatness? How else can we celebrate your fame?

You are indescribable! How can song or tongue describe the measure of your praise?

How can the human mind catch a glimpse of your dazzling throne, where you dwell alone, or probe your unapproachable depths?

The one unknown! All we can know or see have had their birth in you.

Mindful and mindless, all things yield to you, the ultimate parent. We honor and obey you, our life and shield.

Night and day, through our common needs and troubles, all revolve around you. All our prayers end with you.

You put everything in its place, and the universe sings its silent song of majesty to you.

We see how everything draws its life from you, and you have shown your divinity in your design.

You are the goal. One being. All things, yet none.

How do we address you, Mysterious One? Who brings a worthy name? All-named from your own qualities?

How do we speak of you, as you should be spoken of?
You are unlimited, alone. Beyond the range of thought.

How can even a heaven-born intellect part the clouds
above?

Have mercy! Send us a token of your love, Supreme One,
over all. What other name may we use to call on your
greatness, or celebrate your fame?

Amen.

— *Gregory Nazianzen*

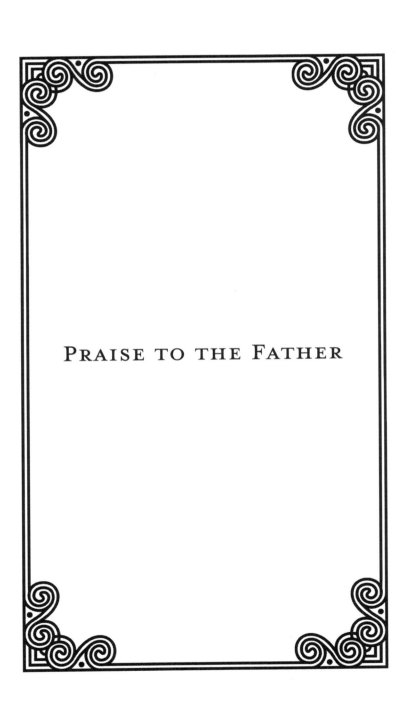

PRAISE TO THE FATHER

WE BOW BEFORE THE HOLY ONE

You alone are the Almighty One. Your eternal power
quenches flames, holds back lions, and tames whales. It
raises up the sick and overrules the power of all things. It
overturns every enemy and brings low the arrogant.

You are the one who is present in heaven, on earth,
in the sea, but you yourself are confined by nothing.
Your majesty has no boundary. As your servant said,
"Acknowledge and take to heart this day that the LORD is
God in heaven above and on the earth below. There is no
other" (Deuteronomy 4:39).

For there is no God besides you alone, there is none holy
besides you, the Lord, the God of knowledge, the God of
the saints, holy above all holy beings, who are sanctified
by your hands.

You are glorious and highly exalted, invisible by nature,
unsearchable in your judgments. Your life is without
want, and your duration can never alter or fail. You do
everything without toil. Your greatness is unlimited. Your
excellency is perpetual.

Your habitation is inaccessible and your dwelling
unchangeable. Your knowledge is without beginning.
Your truth cannot change and you require no help. Your
dominion cannot be taken away and your monarchy will
never have a successor. Your kingdom is without end, your
strength is irresistible, and your army so numerous.

You are the Father of wisdom, the creator of the creation
by a mediator who is also the cause. The bestower of
providence, the giver of laws, the supplier of want, the
punisher of the ungodly, and the rewarder of the righteous.

You are the God and Father of Christ, the Lord of those
devoted to him. Your promise never fails, your judgments
never take a bribe. Your attitude never changes, and your
holiness never ceases.

Our thanksgiving will never end. Let every creature adore
you, for you are worthy, amen.

— *Apostolic Constitutions*

Glory to you for ages to come

Father of your beloved and blessed Son, Jesus Christ, we
have come to know you through him. You are the God
of angels, powers, creation, and the entire race of the
righteous who live in your presence.

I praise you for everything. I bless and glorify you,
through the eternal high priest, Jesus Christ, your beloved
Son, through whom and with him, in the Holy Spirit, be
glory unto you, both now and for the ages to come.

Amen.

— *Polycarp*

I PRAY TO THE FATHER
UNAPPROACHABLE

I pray to you now, Almighty Father, with tears. I have called you unapproachable, incomprehensible, beyond measure.

But I dared not say your Son was inferior to yourself.

I have read that Christ is the radiance of your glory and the exact representation of your being (Hebrews 1:3). And I freely believe that you and your Son and the Holy Spirit are boundless, unmeasurable, inestimable, and indescribable.

If I cannot measure you, Heavenly Father, can I without blasphemy discuss the secrets of your being? Can I say that Christ lacks anything when he himself said "All that belongs to the Father is mine" (John 16:15)?

Scripture says an evil generation seeks a sign, but the only sign we receive is the sign of Jonah (Luke 11:29) ... and the incarnation of Christ.

Who has made me a judge between the Father and the Son, to divide between you and your Son, the glory of uncreated substance?

— *Ambrose of Milan*

I OWE MY LIFE TO YOUR MERCY

Almighty God, there was a time when I, dust and ashes, was not—a time before my life and consciousness and personality began to exist.

I owe my life to your mercy, and I do not doubt that you, in your goodness, gave me my birth for my good. For you, who has no need of me, would never have made the beginning of my life the beginning of evil.

Then, when you had breathed into me the breath of life and endowed me with the power of thought, you instructed me in the knowledge of yourself, by means of the sacred volumes given us through your servants Moses and the prophets.

From them I learned your revelation, that we must not worship you as a lonely God. Their pages taught me of God, not different from you in nature but one with you in mysterious unity of substance. I learned that you are God in God, by no mingling or confusion but by your very nature, since the divinity which is yourself dwells in him who is from you.

But the true doctrine of the perfect birth revealed that you, the Indwelt, and you, the Indweller, are not one person, yet that you dwell in him who is from you.

The voices of evangelists and apostles repeat the lesson, and the very words which fell from the holy mouth of your only-begotten are recorded.

They tell how your Son, God the only-begotten from you the unbegotten God, was born of the virgin as a man to fulfill the mystery of my salvation.

They tell how you dwell in him, by virtue of his true generation from yourself, and he in you, because of the nature given in his abiding birth from you.

Amen.

— Hilary of Poitiers

THAT WE MAY KNOW YOU

I call upon you, Lord God of Abraham, Isaac, Jacob, and Israel. You are the Father of our Lord Jesus Christ, the God who, through the abundance of your mercy, has shown us favor, that we should know you.

You are the one who has made heaven and earth, who rules over all. You are the only and the true God, above whom there is no other.

Amen.

— Irenaeus of Lyons

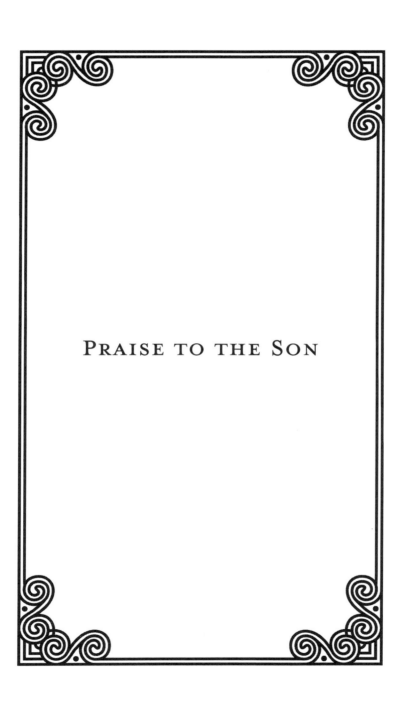

PRAISE TO THE SON

THE THIRD DAY HAS RETURNED

Christ Jesus, you are the Savior of the world, our merciful creator and redeemer, the only offspring from the Godhead of the Father.

Self-existing Word, you are flowing from the heart of God, and powerful from the mouth of your Father, equal to him, of one mind with him, his fellow, of the same age with the Father, from whom at first the world came to be.

You suspend the skies and heap together the soil. You pour forth the seas, which frame all the lands as they flourish.

When you saw our trouble, you became one of us, to rescue us. You were willing not only to be born with a body, but you became flesh, enduring to be born and to die.

You endure funeral rites—you, the author of life and framer of the world! You enter the path of death, in giving the aid of salvation. The gloomy chains of the hellish law yielded, and chaos feared to be pressed by the presence of the light. Darkness perishes, put to flight by your brightness. The thick blanket of eternal night falls away.

Restore the promised pledge, O power of good! The third day has returned; arise, Buried One. It is not proper that your body should lie in the lowly grave. Worthless stone should not hold in the ransom of the world, or cover him in whose fist all things are enclosed. Take away the linen clothes, leave them in the tomb.

You are enough for us, and without you there is nothing. Escape the chains of the evil prison and return to the upper regions. Let us see your face again, that the world may see the light. Give back the day, which flees from us at your death.

You return, holy conqueror! The ruler of the lower regions, who insatiably opens his hollow jaws, becomes your prey. The Lamb pulls his sheep from the jaws of the wolf. You rescue uncounted people from the prison of death, and they follow their leader to freedom. As a warrior you earn back trophies for heaven.

You have restored us from chaos and punishment, given new life to those whom death might seek. You fill your barns with an abundant harvest. Look at your shining triumph, sacred King! We step forth from the bright waves, cleansed and wearing white.

May this people, free from stain, be strengthened in your arms.

Amen!

— *Venantius*

I LONG FOR YOU, SAVIOR

I long for you, Lord of mercy and Lord of my fathers. You have stooped down in grace as a mediator, bringing peace and harmony between heaven and earth.

I seek you, great author of all. With longing I expect you who embrace all with your Word. I wait for you, Lord of life and death.

I look for you, giver and successor of the law. I hunger for you, the one who makes the dead come back to life. I thirst for you, who refreshes the weary. I desire you, creator and redeemer of the world.

You are our God, and we adore you. You are our holy temple, and we pray in you. You are our lawgiver, and we obey you. You are God of all things, the first. God the Father has begotten no other god, and there is no other son who is of one substance and one glory with the Father.

To know you is perfect righteousness, and to know your power is the root of immortality.

For our salvation, you were made the headstone of the corner, precious and honorable. All things are placed under you as their cause and author, as he who brought all things into being out of nothing.

You steer the universe with your wise and steady hand. You are the principle of order and the bond of unity and peace.

In you we live, and move, and have our being. So I will glorify you, my Lord and God. I will praise your name, for you have done wonderful things. From ancient days your wise counsel is faithfulness and truth. You are clothed with majesty and honor.

What is more magnificent than for you, the King, to assume our humanity, illuminating those who sit in darkness and the shadow of death?

Your servant, King David, rightly once sang of you as the King Eternal, saying "you are the most excellent of men" (Psalm 45:2). Coming to the earth, you took on righteousness and faithfulness. Yes, you *are* righteousness and truth, the joy and praise of all.

So we rejoice this day, along with the heavens, for you have shown mercy to your people. Let the clouds drop the dew of righteousness upon the world, and let the earth sound a trumpet blast, for the resurrection is come. I am filled with comfort, and I am overflowing with joy, O Savior of the world!

— *Methodius of Olympia*

A PRAYER TO THE CREATOR CHRIST

You are Jesus Christ, Word of God. Begotten before
the light, creator together with the Father. You are the
fashioner of man, all in all.

Among the patriarchs you are Patriarch; in the law, the Law.
Among the priests, Chief Priest; among kings, the Ruler;
among prophets, the Prophet; among the angels, Archangel.
In the voice of the preacher, you are the Word; among
spirits, the Spirit; in the Father, the Son; in God, God.

You are King forever and ever. For you were the pilot to
Noah, the guide to Abraham, bound with Isaac, in exile
with Jacob, sold with Joseph. You were there with Moses.
In David and the prophets you announced your own
sufferings. You put on bodily form in the Virgin, were
born in Bethlehem, wrapped in swaddling clothes in the
manger, seen by the shepherds, glorified by the angels,
worshiped by the magi.

You were pointed out by John, gathered together the
apostles, and you preached the kingdom. You cured the
lame, gave light to the blind, and raised the dead. You
appeared in the temple, were not believed on by the
people, betrayed by Judas, captured by the priests, and
condemned by Pilate.

You were pierced in the flesh, hung on the tree, and buried in the earth. You rose from the place of the dead, appeared to the apostles, were carried up to heaven, and are seated at the right hand of the Father.

You are the rest for those that are departed, the one who recovers the lost, the light of those who are in darkness, the deliverer of those who are captive, the guide of those who go astray, and the asylum of the afflicted.

You are the bridegroom of the church, the charioteer of the cherubim, and captain of the angels. You are God who is from God, Son from the Father, Jesus Christ the King forevermore.

Amen.

— *Melito of Sardis*

I CANNOT HELP BUT WORSHIP YOU

Lord, what did you do? The sun is not made to shine by
a small lamp. The potter is not molded by the clay. And
the physician is not cured by the sick. The poor receives
contributions from the rich; the rich do not borrow from
the poor.

Can I then be ignorant of who you are, or deny the source
of your light? Because I see my own form in you, am I to
reason against your divine substance, which is invisible
and beyond comprehending? Because you were born here
on earth, just as I was, am I to forget the brightness and
glory of your divinity?

I know you, Lord. I know you clearly. You taught me,
and no one can recognize who you truly are, unless you
illuminate our mind.

The whole of creation adores you, Jesus, and I cannot help
but worship you.

I cannot keep from proclaiming you. Heaven announced
your birth with a star, while choirs of angels praised you
in joy. Shepherds sang to you, their chief shepherd. So
I cannot keep quiet, like the voice of one crying in the
wilderness:

Prepare the way of the Lord!

I am only human, but you are fully God and fully man—
you who were in the beginning, and were with God, and
were God. You are the brightness of the Father's glory, the

perfect image of the perfect Father. The true light who lived among us in the form of a servant, not ashamed to be born at the lowest level of humanity.

You who built the bridge between heaven and earth, do you come to me?

I know how great is the measure of difference between earth and the Creator. I know how great is the distinction between the clay and the potter. I know how superior you are, the Sun of righteousness.

I proclaim your greatness and your perfect lordship, and I am not even worthy to untie your shoelaces. How do I even dare stretch out my hand toward you—you who stretched out the heavens like a curtain and set the earth above the waters?

Extend your right hand toward me, and crown my head by your touch, so that I may run the course before your kingdom, crowned like a forerunner, and announce good tidings to sinners:

Behold the Lamb of God, who takes away the sin of the world!

— *Methodius of Olympia*

MAY I SING FOR YOU?

Christ the Son of God most high, look on me with pity. I come to you as a humble beggar.

Look on me—will you be disappointed, full of sorrow? In your mercy, let me see you, blessed Jesus.

And if someone like me, even me, may appear in your clear glory, in the light you have created, I will worship you in song.

Healer of body and soul, in you may I find my rest, with Father and Spirit, blessed.

Amen.

— Synesius

YOU SHOWED YOUR HEALING POWER

No other power can be found to remedy the evil or the
spirit of injustice that once dominated our race.

But your compassion has reached us where we were and
restored our lives, lives that had been ruined by violence
and immoral living born from human passions.

You displayed your restoration power openly, knowing
that some would recognize and understand. Others would
not. Their brutish natures would lead them to rely only on
the testimony of their own senses.

In the light of day, then, no one would find room for doubt.
You demonstrated your blessed and wonderful healing
power, restored the dead to life, and renewed the crippled
with only a word.

Can we then suppose that rendering the sea as firm
as solid ground, calming the raging storm, and finally
ascending into heaven—all while turning unbelief to faith
by performing these wonders—demanded anything less
than almighty power? Can we believe it was anything less
than the work of God?

O Christ, Savior of humanity, direct the words that
celebrate who you are, and teach me to sound your praises.

Amen.

— Eusebius of Caesarea

Hymn of heaven, take my song

We will sing to you, Deathless One, God himself and God's great Son, creator of endless generations and son of many creations.

You are the God of infinite wisdom, standing among the angels. As man, you mourn among your people. And the magi wondered: Is this newborn child God, or king, or mortal?

We bring our gifts! In the tomb you purified our earth and the rolling tide, the depths below the deep, and even the paths of nations. You are the God who rescues the dead.

Take my music as an anthem from heaven's songs.

Amen.

— *Synesius*

A BLESSING FOR THE ONE

You are the true light who proceeds from the true light, the true God begotten of the true God.

You are the one Lord, before you assumed human form. And you are still that One after you came to earth, ever to be adored.

You are God of your own self, and not by grace. But for our sakes, you are also the perfect man.

In your own nature you are the absolute king and sovereign, but for us and for our salvation existing also in the form of a servant, so that you would make all things uncorrupt.

For yours is the glory, and the power, and the greatness, and the majesty, with the Father and the Holy Spirit forever, amen.

— *Methodius of Olympia*

Your truth stands firm

Will you accept me when I speak this way, Lord? Holiest priest, let this grateful sacrifice rise to you like holy incense.

The power of speech cannot define you, Word of the great mind. You are the high light of the highest light, the only Son, and the image and seal of the Immortal One.

You are without a beginning, from the same fountain of light with the great Spirit. You are infinite in might, and all-glorious, the author of all that is good.

From age to age your truth has stood firm. You reign high in heaven above, almighty breath of mind and Lord of love.

Whatever is or will be—everything throughout the universe is yours. You made it all and give life to all. And you guide us all. There is no fault, strife, or error in your workmanship. Everything is bound back to you.

You laid the foundation of the world, and everything obeys you. You are our sovereign God. For you, the king of the day—the lofty sun—quenches the stars. And as you have commanded, the eye of night—the moon, with its full orb of light—waxes and wanes.

Amen.

— *Gregory Nazianzen*

Brook of heaven, you spring from yourself!

We sing to you, the one who is the great King from all eternity, fountain that springs from itself, God of God, Immortal and Glorious One, the only Father's true and only Son!

To you, with him, our praises all belong. We will crown you with the finest flowers of song. Son of the Father, by divine birth, all the Father's bright glories shine in you.

From you and through the Father comes the Spirit. What a triple mystery! Trinity and unity combined. The sacred fountain was poured into you, yet eternally one.

In the Father's wisdom, mind, and beautiful ray of light, you show us the eternal Son. In you the everlasting purposes shine brightly. You are the beginning of all worlds, bringing shape and form to our bodies.

You command the hosts of heaven, and befriend us here below, overseeing our wandering steps and paths.

You spread your Spirit over the earth, and none of your gifts go to waste. You unchain death's captives, bringing us back to life.

Accept these hymns of praise from me, in your great mercy. Grant me peace, and hold back the tide from this world of trouble—diseases of body and soul, of wealth or poverty—that I may find rest and fill my mind with wisdom from the brook of heaven, amen.

— *Synesius*

PRAISE YOU FOR CREATION

Merciful Creator, you give us life

You are blessed, O Lord, King of ages, who by Christ have made the whole world. By him in the beginning you brought all the disordered parts into order. You divided the waters from the sky and put the spirit of life into them.

You set up the earth, stretched out the heavens, and gave life to every creature.

The world is beautified by your power, Lord. The heavens are fixed as an arch over us, brightened with stars for our comfort in the darkness. The sun was created for days and production of fruit, and the moon for the change of seasons. You brought forth the sky in the midst of the abyss, and commanded the waters to be gathered together, and dry land to appear.

As for the sea itself, waters come with fury—yet they run back again, stopped by the sand at your command. For you have said, "This far you may come and no farther; here is where your proud waves halt" (Job 38:11).

You also made the sea able to support creatures great and small, and navigable for ships. You preserve the courses of shining stars above, and none may depart from your command. They rise and set for signs of the seasons and years.

You created the animals—those belonging to the land, to the water, to the air, and both to air and water. The wisdom you granted them is perfectly suited. You provide for each one.

And at the end of your creation you gave your Wisdom a way, forming a thinking creature as the citizen of the world. "Let us make mankind in our image," you said, "in our likeness" (Genesis 1:26).

Now you present humans as the world's ornament. You have formed them from the elements and prepared a soul from nothing. You gave them senses, and a mind as the conductor of the soul.

O Lord God, who can describe the motion of rainy clouds, the flash of lightning, the noise of thunder—everything that comes together to give us proper food, or a pleasant atmosphere?

But when people were disobedient, you deprived them of the life which should have been their reward. Yet you did not destroy them forever, but laid them to sleep for a time. And by your word you call us to resurrection and loose the bond of death.

You are the reviver of the dead, through Jesus Christ, who is our hope.

Amen.

— *Apostolic Constitutions*

ALL CREATION SINGS YOUR PRAISES

The heavens declare your dominion, O Lord, as the earth shakes. Our globe hangs upon nothing while it proclaims your unshakable steadfastness.

Raging with waves and bound only by the sandy shore, the sea stands in awe at your command, and compels us all to cry out:

"How many are your works, Lord! In wisdom you made them all; the earth is full of your creatures" (Psalm 104:24).

The bright host of angels say, "You are the holy one!" They sing their song of triumph to you forever, saying, "Holy, holy, holy! Heaven and earth are full of your glory!"

Your church here on earth imitates the heavenly choir, with a full heart and a willing soul.

The heavens know who created them, who united land and water, who scattered air to breathe.

The choir of stars admires you as they declare the one who brought them to life.

The animals testify to the one who places the spark of life within them, and trees lift up the one who makes them grow. All creatures, made by your Word, display the greatness of your power.

All here on earth should shout up a hymn from the depth
of our souls to you, through Christ, in the name of all the
created, since you have power over us all, amen.

— Apostolic Constitutions

YOU MADE IT ALL GOOD

O Lord, you have created all things perfect, and nothing
imperfect. To you, no creature is ugly. You have created
them with your divine order, peace, and harmony.

I call to you. Everything that can love, loves you—both
those that know what they love, and those that do not
know what they love.

I call to you who have created all creatures very good,
without any evil, you who will not completely show
yourself to any except the pure in heart.

For you are the Father of truth, the wisdom of the true
and highest life, and the highest life of blessing. You are
the highest good, the highest brightness.

You are the Father of the Son who has awakened us, and
who still brings us to life from the sleep of our sins, and
who bids us come to you.

Amen.

— Augustine of Hippo

CREATION SINGS IN PRAISE

The stars dance for you, Lord, while seasons laugh and sing. Planets shine for you, announcing your wisdom. Your lights sing to the glorious Trinity.

Here below, we too are your glory. We exist to sing your praises, Light of the world.

Immortal One, glory's highest, you took on mortal flesh so you could put an end to our grief.

I live for you, and my songs arise for you. I am a breathing sacrifice, putting aside all the things I once possessed. So I give to you now the only thing remaining:

I will be silent, or sing, at your will. May I do your bidding, either way. May I say what is right, and nothing else. With your guidance, let me see the pearl in the mud, the gold in the sand, the rose in the thorny thicket.

Let me hear what is pure in the noise of life.

Amen.

— *Gregory Nazianzen*

REVERENCE BRINGS ABOUT FAITH

Lord, in this world you have set before us many things whose cause we do not know, but whose effect we can clearly see. And where this kind of ignorance is part of who we are, reverence toward you brings about faith.

When I raise my feeble eyes toward the skies, I know for certain that it is yours. I see in it the paths of the stars, how they move through the seasons: Pleiades and the Big Dipper and the morning star. Each have their appointed places. And I recognize your presence, Lord, in those things in which I cannot gain any clear understanding.

When I watch the amazing movements of your oceans, I know I do not comprehend the origins of the waters, nor the changing currents. Yet I can grasp in faith a reasonable, intelligent cause, even if I cannot see it. I recognize you in these things, though I do not understand them.

I think of the earth itself, which by some hidden power causes seeds to decay, then brings them to life and multiplies them in strength. In all these changes I find nothing my mind can understand, yet my ignorance helps me recognize you. Though I know nothing of nature, I recognize you when I experience these wonders.

So even though I do not understand myself fully, I experience so much that I marvel at you even more *because* of that ignorance. Without understanding fully, my mind can still perceive stars in motion or growing things in the earth—and I owe this ability to you.

You have kept from me the ability to understand my first beginning, yet you still allow me to perceive the charms of nature. And since I recognize you as it concerns me, ignorant as I am, I will have faith in your infinite power. My lack of understanding will not lessen that faith.

I will not attempt to grasp or master the origin of your only-begotten Son, and I will not strain to reach beyond the truth that he is my creator and my God.

Amen.

— *Hilary of Poitiers*

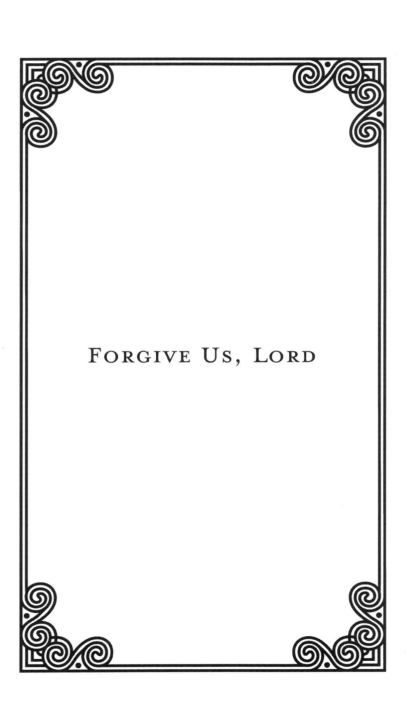

FORGIVE US, LORD

WE BOW OUR SOULS AND BODIES TO YOU

Almighty, eternal God, Lord of the whole world, creator
and governor of all things, you have created us to be
the ornament of the world through Christ. You both
implanted the law on our hearts, and gave it to us in
writing, that we might live according to your standards as
thinking, rational people.

And when we sinned, you gave us your goodness as a
pledge to make a way for our repentance.

Now look down upon us as we bow the neck of our
souls and our bodies to you. You do not want us to die as
sinners. You desire repentance, instead. You want us to
turn from our wicked ways, and live.

You want all people to be saved, and acknowledge the
truth. You once accepted the repentance of the people of
Nineveh. And as in the parable of the prodigal son, where
the father accepted back the son who repented after he
had squandered his inheritance in sinful living—now
would you accept our repentance as we come before you?

For we all sin. But "if you, Lord, kept a record of sins,
Lord, who could stand? But with you there is forgiveness"
(Psalm 130:2–4).

Restore us to your fellowship, in your church. Restore us to
dignity and honor, through Christ our Lord and Savior. By
him be glory and adoration to you, in the Holy Spirit, forever.

Amen.

— *Apostolic Constitutions*

CLEANSE US WITH YOUR TRUTH

Lord, your hand has shown us the everlasting fabric of the world. You created the earth.

You who are faithful throughout all generations, righteous in your judgments, marvelous in strength and excellence...

You who are wise in creating and establishing what you have made...

You who are good, and faithful toward those who trust in you...

You who show pity and compassion...

Forgive us our sins, our unrighteousness, our transgressions, and our shortcomings.

Do not hold us to account for every sin but cleanse us with the cleansing of your truth. Guide our steps to walk in holiness, righteousness, and singleness of heart. Help us to do those things that are good and pleasing in your sight, as well as in the sight of our leaders.

Amen.

— *Clement of Rome*

WASH THE FOOTSTEPS OF MY SOUL

Lord Jesus, you will to wash our feet, as you said to Peter—
and to all the faithful—"Unless I wash you, you have no
part with me" (John 13:8).

Come then, Lord Jesus. Clothe us with your mercy and
your everlasting life. Pour water into the basin, and wash
not only our feet but also our head. And not only the body,
but also the footsteps of my soul.

I want to put off all the filth of my frailty.

As a servant, you washed the feet of your disciples. As
God, you send dew from heaven. And not only do you
wash the feet, but you also invite us to sit down with you,
and you exhort us by saying,

"You call me 'Teacher,' and 'Lord,' and rightly so, for that
is what I am. Now that I, your Lord and Teacher, have
washed your feet, you also should wash one another's feet"
(John 13:13–14).

So I want to wash the feet of my brothers and sisters. I
want to fulfill your command. I will not be ashamed nor
disdain what you did first. This is the mystery of humility:
while washing away the dirt of others, so is my own
washed away.

Amen.

— *Ambrose of Milan*

Help us to forgive others

Lord, do not let us even think of the temporary pleasure
we might get by collecting from those who owe us. Rather,
help us remember the great loss we bring upon ourselves,
from an eternal perspective, when we make those
demands. And how great a loss it is!

Above all, let us forgive those who must give account to
us—both their debts and their offenses. By showing such
mercy, we will receive what we could not gain by our own
virtue or effort.

We gain much by not making our neighbors suffer, and so
we enjoy your eternal blessings by the grace and love you
have shown us in our Lord Jesus Christ.

To you be glory and might now and always, even forever
and forever.

Amen.

—*John Chrysostom*

WE TURN TO YOU

I NEED THE FIRE

Heavenly Father, I need to confess the prophet Isaiah's confession, which he makes before declaring the word of the Lord:

"Woe to me!" he cried. "I am ruined! For I am a man of unclean lips, and I live among a people of unclean lips, and my eyes have seen the King, the Lord Almighty."

If Isaiah said "Woe to me," when he looked upon you, Lord, what do I say of myself? How can I speak of things I fear?

I wish the seraphim would bring a burning coal from the celestial altar, take it in the tongs of the two Testaments, and with that fire purge *my* unclean lips!

But while the seraph came down in a vision to Isaiah, you, O Lord, have revealed the mystery and come to us in the flesh.

You—not by any deputy, nor by any messenger, but you yourself—cleanse my conscience from my secret sins. Then I too, once unclean, but now by your mercy made clean through faith, may sing in the words of David:

"I will praise you with the harp for your faithfulness, O my God; I will sing praise to you with the lyre, O Holy One of Israel. When I sing praise to you my lips will shout for joy, along with my soul, which you have redeemed" (Psalm 71:22–23).

— *Ambrose of Milan*

You invite us to repent

Great are you, O Lord Almighty, and great is your power. Your understanding is infinite.

Our Creator and Savior, you are generously rich, ever-patient, the bestower of mercy. You never take back your salvation from your creatures—because you are by nature good. You spare the sinner and invite us to repent.

Your correction comes from the depths of your compassion. Yet how would we survive if you judged us immediately, today? Because even after so much patience on your part, we can hardly get clear of our miserable condition.

Amen.

— *Apostolic Constitutions*

By your grace I mourn

Preserve your work, Lord. Guard the gift you have given even to those who pulled back.

For I knew I was not worthy to be called your servant, but by your grace I am what I am.

And grant that I may know how with genuine affection to mourn with those who sin. Grant that as often as I learn of the sin of anyone who has fallen, I may suffer with them, and not scold them in my pride, but mourn and weep with them, so that in weeping over another I may also mourn for myself.

Amen.

— *Ambrose of Milan*

WE HAVE SINNED, LORD

We have sinned, Lord, and have gone astray. We have forgotten your commands and chased our own evil thoughts.

We have behaved in a way unworthy of the calling and gospel of your Christ, who suffered and was humiliated for us.

Together we have turned in the wrong direction, cutting short your kindness and your mercies from the depth of your compassion. You are good, you are patient, but we are worthy of punishment.

Who can resist you and the strength of your mighty arm? If you were to shut the heavens, who would open them again? If you let loose your torrents, who could restrain them?

It would be a small thing for you to make poor and make rich, to make alive and to kill, to strike and to heal. And your will is perfect.

We have sinned, and you are angry. We have disgraced even our neighbors. You turned your face; we are filled with shame.

But do not turn away, Lord. Forgive us. We are your people. Correct us in your goodness, not in your anger, so we do not come to nothingness and contempt in the eyes of the entire world.

Amen.

— *Gregory Nazianzen*

Come to my grave and heal

Lord, we show you our wounds so that you may heal us.
And even if we do not, you know, and you wait to hear our
voice. Do away our scars by tears, like the woman in the
Gospel who washed your feet with hers.

You know how to help the weak, when there is no one who
can prepare the feast, or bring the ointment, or carry along
a spring of living water. You come yourself to the grave.

So come to this grave of mine, Lord Jesus, that you would
wash me with your tears. With my dry eyes I have no such
tears as to be able to wash away my offenses. With your
tears I will be saved, if I am worthy of your tears.

With them you will call me out of the tomb of this body
and say, "Come forth." Then my thoughts will not be kept
pent up in the narrow limits of this body, but may go forth
to you, and move into the light, that I may think no more
on works of darkness, but on works of light.

Amen.

— Ambrose of Milan

I WILL SIT AT YOUR TABLE

Call forth your servant, Lord. I am bound with the chain of my sins, my feet fastened and my hands tied, buried in dead thoughts and works.

Yet at your call I will go forth free and will be one of those who are sitting at your feast. Your house will be filled with the aroma of precious ointment.

If you have stooped down to redeem anyone, preserve me. Then they will say about me, See, that person was not brought up in the church, or trained from childhood.

I will be pulled from the fire, away from this world's vanities, to a place where I can hear the choir singing.

And now I will continue serving not in my own strength, but by the grace of Christ, and I will sit among the guests at the heavenly table.

Amen.

— *Ambrose of Milan*

TO WHOM SHOULD I CRY, BUT TO YOU?

Lord, my soul's home is small. Enlarge it, so that you may enter in. It is falling apart; please repair it. It contains that which must offend your eyes—I confess it and know it.

But who will cleanse it? Or to whom should I cry, but to you?

Lord, cleanse me from my secret faults, and spare your servant from the power of the enemy.

I believe, so I speak. Lord, you know.

Have I not confessed to you, against myself, and you, Lord, have forgiven the iniquity of my heart?

I do not contend against your judgment; you are the truth. But I am afraid I will deceive myself, in fear my iniquity might lie to itself. So I do not contend against your judgment.

But if you, Lord, should remember sins, who would survive?

Amen.

— Augustine of Hippo

HEAL ALL OUR BONES

Lord, accept the sacrifice of my confessions from the ministry of my tongue, which you have formed and stirred up to confess your name.

Heal all my bones, and let them say, "Oh Lord, who is like you?"

Those who confess you do not teach you what is inside them. A closed heart does not keep you out, and a person's hard heart cannot hold back your hand. You dissolve it at will, in pity or in vengeance, and nothing can hide from your heat.

But my soul will praise you, and love you. Let my soul confess your mercies, that it may praise you.

Your entire creation does not stop praising you, and it is not silent in your praises. Our weary souls arise toward you, leaning on creation.

That is refreshment. That is true strength.

Amen.

— Augustine of Hippo

RECEIVE ME AGAIN

Merciful, benevolent Lord of kindness—receive me again, your fugitive.

I was once formerly yours, and then fled to the devil. I did his will, and endured misery in his service.

But I have suffered these pains, and have known the shame, long enough. I have served your enemies too long.

Receive me now, Lord, your own servant, for I am fleeing from them. Never let me go back, now that I have sought you. Open to me your door. Teach me how to come.

I have nothing to bring you but good intentions and a desire to love the heavenly and the spiritual above the earthly. And this I do, good Father; I know of nothing better.

But I do not know how to come to you, unless you teach me how. Teach me, then, and help me. If it is by faith that people find you, give me that faith. If it is by any other power, give me that power. If it is by wisdom, give me wisdom.

Grow in me the hope of eternal life, and increase your love in me.

Amen.

— Augustine of Hippo

GRANT US TO LEARN REPENTANCE

Lord Christ, grant to us your servants the blessing of learning the discipline of repentance.

And as we learn repentance, it is also good for us to learn to avoid sin—so we will have no need to repent!

Those who have escaped a shipwreck generally tend to avoid ships and the sea in the future. By keeping fresh the memory of disaster, they honor the second chance you gave them. They honor their deliverance, and are not willing to tempt your mercy all over again.

We have escaped once. Now let us allow ourselves to experience sin's danger that far only—and no farther! Even if it seems that chances are good for us to escape a second time.

Amen.

— *Tertullian*

JESUS, HAVE I LOVED LESS?

Lord Jesus, would you allow me to wash your feet of the
stains you received, walking in me? I wish you would
give me the chance to cleanse the pollution which I by my
deeds have caused on your steps!

But where would I get the living water to wash your feet?
If I have no water, I have tears. And while with them I
wash your feet, I hope I will also be cleansed.

How should you say to me: Your sins (which are many)
are forgiven, because you loved much?

I confess that I owe more, and that more has been forgiven
me. So I fear I may be found ungrateful if I, to whom more
has been given, love less.

Amen.

— Ambrose of Milan

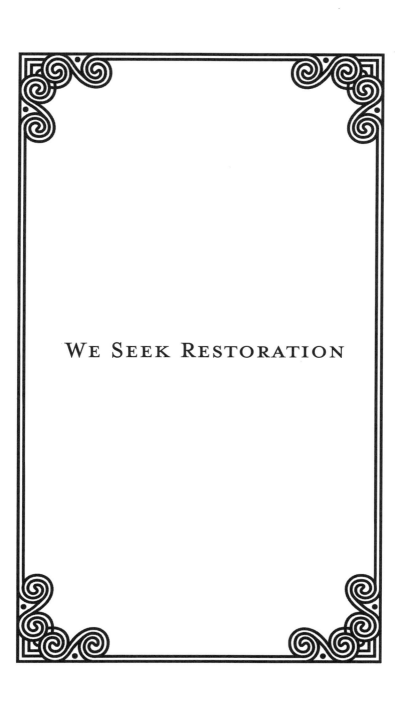

WE SEEK RESTORATION

I WAITED TOO LONG

Late have I loved you, fair God. You are ancient, and yet so new! I waited too long to love you.

For see, you were inside, and I was outside, but I sought you there. Unlovely, I rushed without thinking among the things of beauty you made. You were with me, but I was not with you. And those things kept me far from you, even though they were not at all, unless they were in you.

You called, and you cried aloud, and forced open my deafness.

Your gleam and shine chased away my blindness.

You breathed, and I drew in my breath, panting for you. I tasted you, and now I hunger and thirst.

You touched me, and I yearned for your peace.

Amen.

— Augustine of Hippo

OUR SINS BRING DEEP GRIEF

Our sins bring deep grief!

For it is only when we are not accustomed to them that we pull away.

Once we become used to sin, constant familiarity leads to toleration. And then the habit of toleration leads to the practice of many of them.

This happens, even though the blood of the Son of God was poured out to wash such sins away, and even though they are so great that the kingdom of God is wholly shut against them.

Grant, O Lord, that we may not come to practice all those sins that we are powerless to hold back.

Amen.

— Augustine of Hippo

YOUR GOOD MEDICINE HEALS

You, Lord, abide forever. But you are not angry with us forever, because you pity our dust and ashes. And you were pleased to reform what was deformed in my life.

You brought me awake from the inside out, and made me ill at ease, until I could see you more clearly, inwardly.

By the secret hand of your medicine, my swelling was healed. So was my mind's troubled and dimmed eyesight. Your anointing of healthful sorrows stung, but they brought me to healing, day by day.

Amen.

— *Augustine of Hippo*

WE THANK YOU FOR
LIFE AND BLESSINGS

YOU HAVE GIVEN ME JOY, LORD

Lord, allow me to depart now in peace, according to
your word. "For my eyes have seen your salvation, which
you have prepared in the sight of all nations: a light for
revelation to the Gentiles, and the glory of your people
Israel" (Luke 2:29–32).

You have given me joy, unmixed with pain. Receive me
now, Lord. I rejoice and sing to you of your mercy and
compassion. You have given me this joy of heart, and I
gladly return to you with my thanksgiving tribute.

I have known the power of your love, Lord. For my sake
you became a human—God who is begotten from God, in a
way I cannot describe, in a way that is without corruption.

I have known the inexplicable greatness of your love and
care for us. You sent yourself to deliver us. Now, finally, I
am learning what King Solomon learned:

"Love is as strong as death" (Song of Songs 8:6).

For by love the sting of death is done away. By love the
dead see life. And by love, even death itself will learn what
death is, being made to let go of the dominance it has over
us. By love, also, the serpent—the author of our evils—is
taken captive and overwhelmed.

Amen.

— *Methodius of Olympia*

WE OFFER YOU OUR FIRSTFRUITS

We give thanks to you, O Lord Almighty, creator and preserver of the whole world, through your only begotten Son Jesus Christ our Lord, for the firstfruits which we offer back to you now.

We offer them not as we ought, but as we are able. For who can adequately thank you for everything you have given us?

To the God of Abraham, Isaac, and Jacob—you who made all things fruitful by your word, and commanded the earth to bring forth fruits for our rejoicing and our food—you have given herbs to creatures that feed on herbs, and to some flesh, and to others seeds.

To us you have given grain, and much more—some because we needed it, some for our health, and some for our pleasure.

For your generosity, you are worthy of our highest songs of praise, by Jesus Christ. Glory, honor, and worship be to you, in the Holy Spirit, forever.

Amen.

— Apostolic Constitutions

In creation, show us the Creator

May you who have given us intelligence to recognize your great wisdom in the smallest objects of creation make us find in great bodies a still higher idea of their creator.

Yet, compared with their Author, the sun and moon are just a fly and an ant. The entire universe still cannot give us a right idea of your greatness. It is only by signs, weak and slight in themselves, often by the help of the smallest insects and of the least plants, that we raise ourselves to you.

Content with these words, we offer our thanks. In proportion to our faith may you grant us your Spirit in Jesus Christ our Lord, to whom be glory and power forever and ever.

Amen.

— Basil of Caesarea

KEEP US FAITHFUL TO YOUR TRUTH

The sea is good in your eyes, Lord. It circles the islands, giving both protection and beauty. It brings together the most distant parts of the earth, and gives ships a path on which to sail from port to port. So it gives us a way to communicate, supplies the merchant with wealth, allows the rich to export, and blesses the poor with the supply of what they lack.

But how should I see the ocean's goodness in your eyes, Creator? If the ocean is good and praiseworthy in your eyes, how much more beautiful is the assembly of a church! Here, the voices of men, women, and children arise in prayers to you, mingling and resounding like the waves that beat on the shore.

This church also enjoys a profound calm, and the breath of heresy is not found here. As we remain faithful to the truth we receive your approval in our Lord Jesus Christ, to whom be glory and power for ever and ever.

Amen.

— *Basil of Caesarea*

WE REAP THE EVERLASTING FRUIT OF YOUR GOODNESS

We give you thanks, our God and Savior, and to you, O Christ, in our own feeble way. You are the supreme providence of the mighty Father, who both saves us from evil and teaches us in the way of truth.

I say these things not to praise, but simply to give thanks. Who among us is worthy to give you praise? You called creation into being from nothing. You illuminated it with your light. You regulated the confusion of the elements by your laws of harmony and order.

More than that, we recognize your lovingkindness. You caused those whose hearts inclined toward you to sincerely seek a divine and blessed life. You've allowed us to pass along what we've received from you, like merchants of wisdom and true blessings.

We reap the everlasting fruit of your goodness. Freed from the net of sin, and permeated with a love for others, mercy is always our point of view.

We hope for the promise of faith, and we are devoted to modest living—all the virtues we had once thrown aside, but are now restored by you whose generous care is over all.

Amen.

— *Eusebius of Caesarea*

YOU ARE THE BREATH OF HEAVEN

Our Lord and God, the sweet fragrance and the sweetness of your love breathes in us.

Our souls are lit up through the knowledge of your truth.

Make us worthy to receive the outpouring of your beloved from heaven. We will give you thanks in that place.

Meanwhile, we will glorify you without ceasing in your church. You are crowned and filled with every blessing because you are Lord and Father, creator of all.

Amen.

— Adæus and Maris

WE THANK YOU FOR
THE INCARNATION

MEDIATOR, WE GIVE YOU GLORY

Glory to you who clothed yourself in the body of mortal Adam, and made a fountain of life for all mortals.

You are the one who lives, and those who killed you were actually like gardeners, sowing your life like a seed of wheat in the depths of the earth, so that it could rise and raise up many with it.

Lord, may our love be now like a sweet offering, and may the hymns and prayers of your people rise up to you who made your own offering on the cross, an offering on behalf of all humanity.

You stooped down from above to us below, so you could pass along your treasures to us. You became the treasurer of your riches, bringing your gifts from the storehouse and distributing them to the needy.

We give you glory, our Mediator. For through you we receive life, just as we once received death from the one who would slay us.

Amen.

— *Ephraim the Syrian*

YOU ARE THE JOY OF ALL

By coming to earth as a human, you equipped yourself
with righteousness. You anointed yourself with
faithfulness. You yourself are righteousness and truth. You
are the joy of all. We lift you high!

So I tell the heavens to rejoice with me today, for you have
showed mercy to your people. Let the clouds drop the
dew of righteousness on the world. Let the foundations
of the earth sound a trumpet blast to the dead for the
resurrection to come.

May compassion also spring up for all people of this earth. I
am overjoyed since I have met you, Jesus, the Savior of all!

Amen.

— *Methodius of Olympia*

WE GIVE THANKS TO
THE TRIUNE GOD

You are the eternal Father, eternal Son

As long as I have the power by means of the Spirit which you have given me, Holy Father, Almighty God, I will confess that you are not only eternally God, but also eternally Father.

I will never make the great mistake of presuming to judge your infinite power or your mysteries. On account of my weak understanding, I will not arrogantly seek more than what I have learned: a devoted belief in your infinite nature, and faith in your eternity.

I will not claim that you were ever without your wisdom, power, or Word—without the only-begotten God, my Lord Jesus Christ.

Our own weak and imperfect language, which limits us, does not dominate my thoughts about you, Lord. My language poverty will not choke faith into silence.

For though we are given an inward freedom of word, wisdom, and power, your perfect Word, Wisdom, and Power come from a perfect God—and he can never be separated from yourself. In these names your eternal properties are shown to be born of you.

Yet his birth—the birth of our Lord Jesus—is only shown to prove that you are the source of his being. It is enough to confirm our belief in his infinity, since he was born before times eternal.

Amen.

— *Hilary of Poitiers*

You are always, before eternity

Father, the birth of our Lord Jesus is before times eternal.

If anything exists before eternity, it will be something which, when eternity is comprehended, still eludes comprehension.

And this something is yours—your only-begotten. He is not a portion, he is not an extension, and he is not an empty name devised to suit some theory of how you acted.

He is the Son, a Son born of you, God the Father, himself true God, begotten by you in the unity of your nature.

He is properly acknowledged after you, and yet with you, since you are the eternal author of his eternal origin.

And since he is from you, he is second to you. Yet since he is yours, you are not to be separated from him.

For we must never assert that you once existed without your Son—otherwise we would be blaming you of being less than perfect before Jesus, or superfluous after Jesus.

So the exact meaning for us of the *eternal generation* is that we know you to be the eternal Father of your only-begotten Son, who was born of you before times eternal, amen.

— *Hilary of Poitiers*

I cannot limit the Spirit

Father, I cannot describe the one whose pleas for me I also cannot describe.

Since Scripture tells us that your only begotten was born of you before times eternal, so when we give up struggling with the ambiguities of language and difficulties of thought, one certainty of his birth remains.

So I hold fast in my mind the truth that your Holy Spirit is from you and through Christ, although I cannot comprehend it. I am dull in spiritual things.

As your only begotten one says, "You should not be surprised at my saying, 'You must be born again.' The wind blows wherever it pleases. You hear its sound, but you cannot tell where it comes from or where it is going. So it is with everyone born of the Spirit" (John 3:7–8).

Though I believe my regeneration is real, Lord, I do so in ignorance. I possess the reality, but I don't comprehend it. My own consciousness had no part in causing this new birth, which is displayed in its results.

The Spirit has no limits, either. He speaks whatever, whenever, and wherever he wants. Should I believe the Spirit is created, and limit him by counting a time of his origin?

John writes that all things were made through the Son. As God, the Word was in the beginning with you. And Paul recounts that all things were created in Christ, things in heaven and earth, visible and invisible. But with respect to the Holy Spirit, he thought it was enough to simply call him your Holy Spirit.

So I will agree with these men, your elect. Following their example, I will say nothing beyond my comprehension about your only begotten, but simply declare that he was born. And again following their example, I will not trespass beyond what human intellect can know about your Holy Spirit, but simply declare that he is your Spirit.

I desire no useless war of words, only a confession that never wavers of a faith that never hesitates, amen!

— *Hilary of Poitiers*

WE THANK YOU FOR
SALVATION IN CHRIST

YOU HAVE NOT FORGOTTEN US

I will rejoice, Lord, singing of your mercy and
compassion. You have given me this joy of heart. I gladly
give you my thanks.

I have known the power of your love. For my sake you
became a perfect man.

I have known the indescribable greatness of your love and
care for us. From the depths of your care, you came to
deliver us.

Now I finally understand what I had learned from
Solomon: "Love is as strong as death, its jealousy
unyielding as the grave. It burns like blazing fire, like a
mighty flame" (Song of Songs 8:6).

Lord, you have unveiled your salvation to us. You have
caused the plant of peace to grow for us. We will no longer
wander aimlessly.

You let us know that you have not forgotten us. You have
not forgotten your creation. Out of compassion for our
low position, you pour on us your inexhaustible goodness.
You yourself redeemed us through your only begotten
Son—who is unchangeably like you and of one substance
with you. You did not leave the work of salvation to a
servant or even a minister.

You have given the light to those who sat in darkness
and in the shadow of death. Now we see the light of
knowledge. And you fashioned us again into everlasting

life, through our Lord and creator. You have graciously brought us back to paradise through the one who first separated humanity from paradise.

Amen.

— Methodius of Olympia

YOU FREED US FROM THE FEAR OF DEATH

You, O Lord, have freed us from the fear of death. You have made the end of this life the beginning to us of true life.

For a season, you rest our bodies in sleep, and awaken them again at the last trumpet call. You give our earth, which you fashioned with your hands, to the earth to keep in safety.

One day you will take again what you have given, transfiguring with immortality and grace our mortal and unpleasant remains.

You have saved us from the curse and from sin, having become both for our sakes. You broke the head of the dragon that had seized us in his jaws, in the yawning gulf of disobedience.

You have shown us the way of resurrection, having broken the gates of hell, and you brought to nothing the one who had the power of death—the devil.

You have given a sign to those who fear you—the cross, to destroy the adversary and save our lives.

Amen.

— Gregory of Nyssa

In you we live

You are the one who was made the headstone of the corner—for our salvation!

You are precious and honorable. All things take their place under you as their cause and author. You are the one who brought all things into being, out of nothing.

You are the connector and preserver of all created things, the framer of all. You steer the universe with your wise and steady hand. You are the very principle of all good order. The unbreakable bond of harmony and peace.

In you we live, and move, and have our being.

So I will glorify you, O Lord my God. I will praise your name. You have done wonderful things. Your age-old wisdom is faithfulness and truth. You wear majesty and honor like clothing.

For what is more brilliant for a king than a robe embroidered with flowers, and a shining crown? You delight in the people you have created. What is more magnificent for you than to take on our form? You light up those who sit in darkness, in the shadow of death.

How right did that earthly king, your servant, once sing of you as the eternal King, saying you are "fairer than the sons of men" (Psalm 45:2 KJV).

Amen.

— *Methodius of Olympia*

WE ARE REMADE

You have shown us, Lord, the salvation that makes a plant of peace spring up. We will no longer wander in error.

You have made known to us, Lord, that you have not overlooked us. You have not forgotten your creation, the work of your hands.

For out of your compassion for our lowliness, you have poured out on us your abundant, inexhaustible goodness. You have redeemed us through your only begotten Son, who is forever and always one with you.

You judged it unworthy of your majesty to entrust to anyone else the work of saving and lifting up your servants.

With that light, which is the same substance as you, you have given light to those who sat in darkness, in the shadow of death, so that "in your light we see light" (Psalm 36:9).

Through our Lord and creator, you have seen fit to remake us unto eternal life, and you have graciously allowed us to return to paradise by means of him who had separated us from the joys of paradise.

Through him who has the power to forgive sins, you have blotted out the handwriting that was against us.

Amen.

— *Methodius of Olympia*

YOU OPENED THE PRISON, LORD

Surely, Lord, you are the pure and eternal fountain of goodness. You were right to turn away from us, and in lovingkindness you had mercy on us.

You hated, and were reconciled. You cursed, and blessed. You banished us from paradise, and called us back. You stripped off the fig leaves—an unattractive covering—and put on us an expensive garment.

You opened the prison, and released the condemned. You sprinkled us with clean water, and cleansed us from our filthiness.

Adam will no longer be bewildered when you call. He will no longer hide himself, convicted by his conscience, cowering in the thicket of paradise. The flaming sword will no longer surround paradise, cutting off the entrance to those who draw near.

All is now turned to joy for those of us who were once heirs of sin. We can now walk in paradise—heaven itself. And the creation once in conflict with itself, in the world and above the world, is now knit together in friendship.

We humans now join in the angels' song, offering worship of praise to God. For all these things let us sing to God that hymn of joy—a song which lips touched by the Spirit long ago sang loudly:

"I delight greatly in the Lord; my soul rejoices in my God. For he has clothed me with garments of salvation and arrayed me in a robe of his righteousness, as a bridegroom adorns his head like a priest, and as a bride adorns herself with her jewels" (Isaiah 61:10).

And surely the one who adorns the bride is Christ, who was, and is, and will be blessed now and for evermore.

Amen.

— *Gregory of Nyssa*

WE THANK YOU FOR TIME
TO WORSHIP AND REST

A PRAYER OF THANKS AFTER
COMMUNION

We thank you, Holy Father, for your holy name which you have caused to live in our hearts, and for what you have made known to us of faith and eternal life through Jesus your servant. We give you glory forever!

You, almighty Master, created all things for the sake of your name. You gave us food and drink to enjoy, so we might give you thanks. You also freely gave us spiritual food and drink, and eternal life through Jesus.

We thank you for being mighty, Lord. Remember your church, to deliver it from all evil and to make it perfect in your love. Gather us together from the four winds, set apart as holy for the kingdom you have prepared. Yours is the power and the glory forever.

Let grace come, and let this world pass away. Loud praises to the God and Son of David! Come quickly, Lord.

Amen.

— Apostolic Constitutions

Gather your church into your kingdom

Our Father, we thank you for the life you have made known to us by Jesus your Son. By him you made all things, and by him you take care of the whole world.

You permitted your Son to suffer and die, then you raised him up and glorified him, setting him down on your right hand.

By him you have promised us the resurrection of the dead.

Lord Almighty, everlasting God, gather your church into your kingdom from the ends of the earth, as grain was once scattered, and has now become one loaf of bread.

Father, we also thank you for the precious blood of Jesus Christ, shed for us, and for his precious body, the church. We celebrate this representation, as Scripture tells us, "to proclaim the Lord's death" (1 Corinthians 11:26).

For through him glory is to be given to you forever.

Amen.

— Apostolic Constitutions

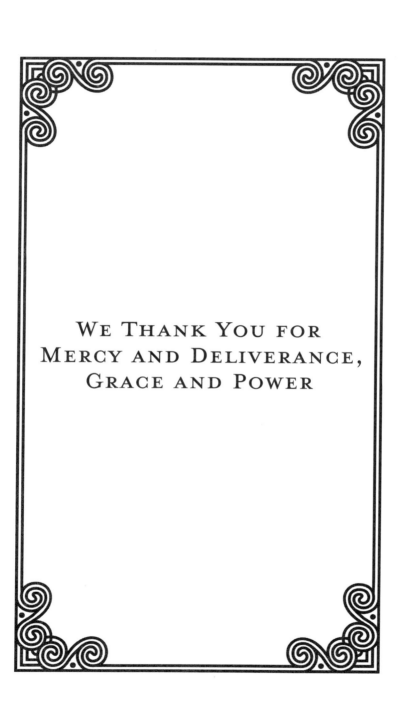

WE THANK YOU FOR
MERCY AND DELIVERANCE,
GRACE AND POWER

This is gracious rain

Lord Jesus, this is the special excellence of your lovingkindness: you redeem the whole world, one soul at a time.

Elijah was sent to one widow. Elisha cleansed one. You, Lord Jesus, cleanse a thousand in a day.

How many in our cities? How many have you cleansed there? How many have you cleansed today, in the entire world?

We do not cleanse anyone. Ours is the ministry, but it is not within our power to pass along what is divine. It is your gift, Lord, and the Father's. As you spoke by the prophets,

"I will pour out my Spirit on all people. Your sons and daughters will prophesy..." (Joel 2:28).

This is what dew from heaven is like, Lord. This is gracious rain. As the Scriptures tell us, "You gave abundant showers, O God; you refreshed your weary inheritance" (Psalm 68:9).

For your Holy Spirit is not subject to any foreign power or law, but he is the judge of his own freedom, deciding all things according to his own will, to each individually as he wills.

Amen.

— *Ambrose of Milan*

WE GIVE YOU THANKS, MIGHTY ONE!

We give thanks to you, Father, for your holy name which you made to dwell in our hearts. Thank you for the knowledge, faith, and immortality which you made known to us through Jesus your Son. To you be glory forever.

You, Lord Almighty, created all things for your name's sake, and gave people food and drink for their enjoyment, that they might give thanks to you. And you have blessed us with spiritual food and drink and eternal light through your Son.

Above all we give thanks to you that you are mighty. To you be glory forever.

Remember your church, Lord, to deliver it from all evil and to make it perfect in your love, and gather it together in its holiness from the four winds to your kingdom which you have prepared for it. For yours is the power and the glory forever.

Let grace come and let this world pass away. Hosanna to the God of David. If any one is holy, let them come! If any one be not, let them repent.

Maranatha—our Lord, come!

Amen.

—The Didache

YOU SHOWED US THE WAY OF RESURRECTION

Lord, you have freed us from the fear of death. You have made the end of this life the beginning to us of true life.

For a season you rest our bodies in sleep and awaken them again at the last trumpet. You give our earth, which you have fashioned with your hands, to the earth to keep in safety. One day you will take again what you have given, transfiguring with immortality and grace our mortal and unsightly remains.

You have saved us from the curse and from sin, having become both for our sakes. You have broken the heads of the dragon who had seized us in his jaws, in the yawning gulf of disobedience.

You have shown us the way of resurrection, having broken the gates of hell, and brought to nothing him who had the power of death, the devil.

You have given a sign to those who fear you: the symbol of the cross, to destroy the adversary and save our life.

O God eternal, I have been attached to you from my mother's womb. My soul has loved you with all its strength. I have dedicated to you both my flesh and my soul, from my youth up until now. Give me now an angel of light to guide me to the place of refreshment, where there is the water of rest, in the bosom of the holy fathers.

You who broke the flaming sword and restored to paradise the man that was crucified with you and begged for your mercies—remember me, too, in your kingdom. Because I, too, was crucified with you. My flesh was nailed to the cross in awe and reverence of you.

I have feared your judgments. Do not let a terrible chasm separate me from those you have chosen. Do not allow the slanderer to stand in my way. And do not let my sin be found before your eyes—if in anything I have sinned in word, thought, or deed, led astray by the weakness of our nature.

You who have the power on earth to forgive sins, forgive me, so that I am refreshed and may be found before you when I put off my body, without defilement on my soul. May my soul be received into your hands spotless and undefiled, as an offering before you.

Amen.

— Macrina (recorded by her brother, Gregory of Nyssa)

WE WILL NOT TURN AWAY FROM YOU

Lord our God, you have become our refuge from
generation to generation.

You were our refuge, so we might be born—those who
once were not.

You were our refuge, so that we might be born anew—
those who once were evil.

You were a refuge to feed those who turned away from you.

You are a refuge to raise up and direct your children. You
have become our refuge.

We will not turn away from you, when you have delivered
us from all our evils and filled us instead with your good
things. You give good things now, and you are gentle
with us, so we do not grow weary in the way. You correct,
reprimand, discipline, and direct us, so we may not
wander from the way.

But whether you deal gently with us (so we will not grow
weary in the way) or correct us (so we will not wander
from the way), you have become our refuge, O Lord.

Amen.

— *Augustine of Hippo*

NOW I KNOW

My Lord, let me remember with gratitude and confess to you your mercies toward me.

Soak my bones in your love, and let them say: "Lord, who is like you?"

You have burst my chains, and I will offer a sacrifice of thanksgiving to you.

I will declare how you set me free. And when they hear these things, all who worship you will say, "Blessed be the Lord in heaven and earth. Great and wonderful is his name!"

Your words are planted permanently inside me. You have surrounded me on every side. And I am now made certain of your eternal life, where once I saw "only a reflection as in a mirror" (1 Corinthians 13:12).

Amen.

— Augustine of Hippo

ETERNITY IS NOT ENOUGH TO THANK YOU

We give you thanks for all things, O Lord Almighty, for not taking away your mercies and compassion from us. In every passing generation you save and deliver, help, and protect.

You helped in the days of Enos and Enoch, of Moses and Joshua. You helped in the days of the judges, of Samuel and Elijah and the prophets, in the days of David and the kings, in the days of Esther, Mordecai, and Judith, in the days of Judas Maccabeus and his brothers.

You helped in our own days by your great high priest, Jesus Christ your Son. He has delivered us from the sword, from sickness, and from famine. He has sustained us and preserved us from evil.

We give you thanks for all this through Jesus Christ, who has given us a voice to confess him, sight to contemplate him, even hearing and smell. He has given us hands for working and feet for walking.

And all this you formed from a little drop in the womb, upon which you bestowed an immortal soul, and brought us into light as rational creatures.

You taught and improved us by your laws. And from temporary death you promise resurrection. What life is enough, or what length of ages will be long enough, for people to be thankful?

We cannot thank you enough, but it is just and right to do so as we are able. For you have delivered us from the grave mistake of worshiping many gods, and from the heresies of those who oppose Christ. You have delivered us from ignorance and error.

You sent Christ among men as a man, being the only begotten God. You sent the Comforter to live among us. You set angels over us and put the devil to shame. You brought us into being when we were not, and you care for us. You measure out life to us, and give us food.

We glorify and worship you for all these things, through Jesus Christ, now and forever, through all ages, amen.

— *Apostolic Constitutions*

You know me best

If I am truly wise, I should now rejoice in the place that
you, O Christ, have approved for me. After all, you are
preparing far better things now than I had before.

Before, I thought your approval meant prosperity.
Before, my home was abundant in luxury. Before, I
flourished in status amidst throngs of crowds and clients.

I now regret that I once loved all those things that were
doomed to perish. But with old age I finally recognize
(to my profit) that by the loss of earthly and failing riches
I might learn to seek rather those things which will endure
forever.

It is indeed late, O God. But nothing is ever too late
with you.

You will always show compassion. And you know how
to help those who do not know how to help themselves—
because you anticipate our prayers even before we ask,
and you provide good things for us beyond what we seek.

You also refuse many selfish, misguided prayers, though
you are ready to grant even better things to those wise
enough to prefer your gifts to their own wishes.

For how much better did you know me and my character—
better than I did myself. You saw when I stepped out
on a task that was beyond my strength.
You gave me something better, by blocking my plans.

By your mighty hand and foreseeing power, you directed
all things.

Amen.

— Paulinus Pellaeus

YOU PRESERVE US IN MERCY

O Lord our mediator, you are God above us and man
for us.

I own your mercy!

Though you are so great, you take the time to preserve all
those many people in your body who are troubled by their
own ongoing experience of weakness.

Through the good will of your love and the richness of
your comfort, you keep them from utterly perishing in
their despair.

Amen.

— Augustine of Hippo

Make my heart steadfast

As I rejoice in your great and generous gifts to me, Almighty God, I owe you fresh thanks—even thanks that would overshadow and bury all those I have given you before.

And though my constant devotion may have gone too far, and nearly calls upon itself to pause, still it does not know how to stop dwelling on the gifts I owe you, O Christ.

This I make my only good, this I must hold fast, this with my whole heart I long to secure, in all places, everywhere, and continually at all times: In utterance, that I would tell of you. And in silence, that I would remember you.

I owe you all of myself and everything I own, most excellent God. As I began this life from you, so in finishing it I end … to you.

And while I have often asked you earnestly, now much more fervently I beg you. Since at this old age I see nothing else to fear but death, and I cannot recall anything else I could want, whatever you will, please grant me an unflinching heart in the face of sorrow.

I have followed your way for years, and I seek to win your promise of salvation. Now make my heart steadfast by the gift of your power, so that I may not dread the hour of death. That hour is now nearer on account of my advanced age, though every season of life is subject to you.

In my change-filled life, Lord, may no random events
cause me to doubt and fear. Whatever awaits me at the
end, let the hope of seeing you, O Christ, relieve those
fears. May they be avoided under your leadership—
dispelled by the sure confidence that while I am still in this
mortal body, I am yours (since everything is yours). And
when I am released from this body, I will also be in some
part of yours.

Amen.

— *Paulinus Pellaeus*

GREAT IS YOUR PATIENCE, LORD

Great is your patience, Lord, full of compassion and grace.
You are slow to anger and abundant in mercy. You are
true!

You make the sun rise on both good and evil, and send
rain on the just and unjust. Your desire is not for the death
of sinners, but that they return and live. You make room
for repentance, that they would abandon sin and believe
in you.

Your patience leads to repentance, though many still store
up wrath for themselves through hardness of heart. Then
your righteous judgment is revealed and you will deal with
us all according to what we have done (Romans 2:4–6).

But you forget all our iniquities when we turn from sin to
your mercy and truth.

Grant that many more may be liberated through the
sacrifice of a broken spirit and a contrite and humbled
heart, in the sorrow of repentance.

For nothing matters except your surpassing mercy and
power, the truth of your baptism, and the keys of the
kingdom of heaven in your church. We will not give up on
anyone as long as, by your patience, they still live on this
earth.

—*Augustine of Hippo*

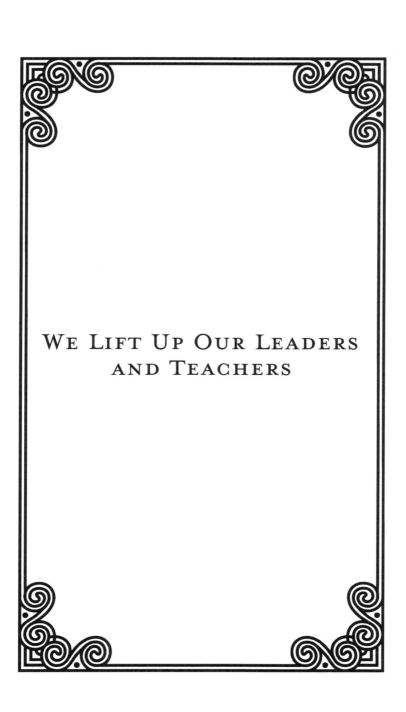

WE LIFT UP OUR LEADERS AND TEACHERS

GUARD THE SHEPHERD OF THIS FLOCK

Ruler and Lord of all, Father and God, guard the shepherd of this flock.

You are the cause and the power. You are the helper; we are the ones who need your help. You are the physician, the savior, and the wall around us. You are the life, the hope, the refuge, the joy, the expectation, and our rest. You are all things to us.

We need you in order to be eternally saved. We·need you to preserve and protect. You can do all things, for you are the ruler of rulers, the Lord of lords, the governor of kings.

Give power to this our leadership to loose what should be loosed, and bind what should be bound. Make our leaders wise, and through them protect the church of Jesus as you would a fair bride.

For your glory is forever. In you we offer our praise forever to the Father, Son, and Holy Spirit.

Amen.

— *Clement of Rome*

STRENGTHEN OUR PASTOR

Lord, strengthen our pastor to guard the sheep that are whole, visit those who are sick, bind up those who are broken, and seek out those who are lost.

Help him to feed these sheep in the pastures of the Scriptures, and to give us a drink from the spring of doctrine, of understanding who you are. May the truth be a wall around us, and truthfulness, peace. And may the cross be a staff for this shepherd.

Give him the power of David, who plucked a straying lamb from the mouth of the lion. In the same way, give him strength to snatch from the evil one the souls that are precious above all. Nothing but the blood of Christ can buy them.

May the fountain of your words flow from him, that he might become a harp for the Spirit.

Blessed be the one who was sold and bought us all! Blessed be the one who has sowed unity among us.

Amen.

— *Ephraim the Syrian*

POUR YOUR SPIRIT ON YOUR SERVANTS

Lord God Almighty, no one rules over you. You always were, and are, and will be. You stand in need of nothing.

You alone are true, and wise, and most high. You alone are good, and beyond compare. Your knowledge is without beginning.

You are God and Father of your only begotten Son, of our God and Savior, the creator of the whole world by him. Your providence provides for and takes care of all.

Father of mercies, God of all consolation, you dwell in the highest heaven, but see us here below.

From the beginning, you ordained leaders for your people: Abel, Seth, and Amos. Enoch and Noah. Melchizedek and Job. Abraham and the rest of the patriarchs, with your faithful servants Moses and Aaron, Eleazar and Phineas … who chose rulers and priests in the tabernacle.

Pour down the influence of your Spirit. Grant by your name that this servant whom you have chosen may feed your flock, serving you night and day, and gathering those who will be saved.

May he please you in meekness and a pure heart, with a steadfast and blameless mind, above reproach, offering to you a pure sacrifice through Jesus Christ, our God and Savior.

All glory, honor, and worship be to you in the Holy Spirit, now and always, and for all ages, amen.

— *Apostolic Constitutions*

A PRAYER FOR OUR RULERS

Lord, make your face shine on us in peace and for our good, that we may be sheltered by your mighty hand and delivered from every sin by your uplifted arm.

Deliver us from those who hate us wrongfully.

Grant us peace, and peace to all those around us, as you did in the past when your people called on you in faith and truth, living holy lives.

We bow in obedience before your almighty and excellent name, and we also submit to our rulers and governors here on the earth.

Lord and Master, you have given these rulers the power of sovereignty through your own mighty power. And as we understand the honor you have given them, help us to submit ourselves and not resist your will in any way. Grant unto these leaders health, peace, unity, and stability, so they can administer without failure the government you have given them.

For you—Heavenly Master and King of the Ages—you give ordinary people glory, honor, and power over all things in this world. Direct their leadership in a way that is good and well pleasing in your sight. Gently and peacefully administer the power you have given them, with godliness, and may they receive your favor.

To you who alone are able to do these things for us, and far more besides, we praise you through the high priest and guardian of our souls, Jesus Christ. Through him be the glory and majesty unto you, both now and for all generations, forever and ever, amen.

— *Clement of Rome*

GIVE STRENGTH AND POWER TO YOUR PEOPLE

God of peace, who has restored us to each other, and made the two one:

You who set kings upon thrones, who raise the poor out of the dust, and lift up the beggar from the dung hill.

You who chose David and took him away from the sheepfolds, though he was the least and youngest of the sons of Jesse.

You who gave the word to those who preach the gospel with great power for the perfection of the gospel.

Hold me by my right hand, guide me with your counsel, and receive me with glory.

You who are a shepherd to shepherds and a guide to guides, help us to feed your flock with knowledge, not with the instruments of a foolish shepherd.

Help us to serve according to the blessing, and not according to the curse pronounced against the men of former days.

Give strength and power to your people. Present your flock dazzling and spotless, worthy of the fold on high, in the place of rejoicing and in the splendor of the saints.

Do this so that in your temple everyone, both flock and shepherds, together may say: Glory in Christ Jesus our Lord, to whom be all glory forever and ever!

Amen.

— *Gregory Nazianzen*

GIVE YOUR SERVANTS A NEW HEART

Lord God Almighty, God who is unbegotten and inaccessible, you are the only true God, the God and Father of your Christ, your only begotten Son, God of the Comforter and Lord of the whole world.

By Christ, you appointed your disciples to teach true devotion to you. Now look down upon your servants who are being trained in the gospel of your Christ. Give them a new heart, and renew a right spirit in their inward parts, so that they may both know and do your will with full purpose of heart and with a willing soul.

Unite them with your body, the church set apart, and allow them to know your deep truths, through Christ, who is our hope and who died for them. And we give you glory and worship through Jesus Christ in the Holy Spirit forever.

Amen.

— *Apostolic Constitutions*

PURIFY THE EARS OF OUR LEADERS

Come to us, Lord, and purify the ears of our leaders. Purge my ears, as well, that no stains would remain from all the infidelity they have heard.

Cleanse our ears thoroughly, not with water from a well or from a river, but with words cleansing like water, but clearer than any water, and purer than any snow—as you have said:

"Though your sins are like scarlet, they shall be as white as snow" (Isaiah 1:18).

Cleanse the spiritual ears of our leaders, so they may love peace, show loving patience, and have no contempt for that which is sacred.

May they elevate the importance of faith, as it is written, "Sell all that you have. ... Then come, follow me" (Luke 18:22).

Purify our senses that we may adore and worship you, Creator of all things visible and invisible.

Amen.

—*Ambrose of Milan*

LET ME ONLY TEACH YOUR TRUTH

Lord, from your bread give me words to answer those
in your family who may not hunger and thirst for
righteousness, but who are already full from a poor copy
that is not your truth.

I certainly know how many fabrications the human heart
can give birth to. My own heart is a human heart! But,
God of my heart, I pray that I would not pass off any
fabrications as solid truths.

Let me only teach what the breath of your truth has
breathed into me—even if I were cast off from the sight of
your eyes, striving from a distance to return by the path
which the divinity of your only begotten Son has made for
us through his humanity.

I drink in your truth, changeable though I am. And I see
nothing changeable in your truth: neither in place nor in time.

For your essence has nothing at all that is changeable—not
in eternity, nor in truth, nor in your will. Your truth and
your love are eternal. Your love is true, and eternity true.

Amen.

— *Augustine of Hippo*

WE DEDICATE OUR WORK TO YOU

Look on our efforts and prayers, Lord, and prosper our work. We dedicate it all to you.

Fill our words with the fruit of the gospel, and grant that this may become holy and saving food for all the people of your church, for people of all ages.

And if there are some who are affected by the deadly breath of that poisonous serpent—if some have become ill in their weakened condition—give them robust health and sound faith.

Grant them, through these words, the saving care of your gift. Just as the five loaves and two fishes were completely set apart by you, so may hungry souls be strengthened as they eat our words.

In that way, and as they eat, would you cause those who need spiritual energy to be healed?

Amen.

—John Cassian

WE REMEMBER OUR
CONGREGATION

COME TO THIS WEDDING FEAST

Lord Jesus, come to your church, completely and fully. Send out the word to the highways. Gather everyone, good and bad. Bring the weak, the blind, and the lame into your church. Bring everyone to your supper. Command that your house be filled!

You will make worthy everyone who follows you. We are rejected without the wedding garment, however—the clothes of your compassion, the veil of your grace. I pray that you would provide that garment for everyone.

Your church does not excuse herself from the supper. Your family does not say, "I am whole, I do not need the physician." Instead, we say: "Heal me, O Lord, and I will be healed; save me, and I will be saved."

Your church is like that woman who went behind and touched the hem of your garment, saying to herself: "If I just touch his clothes, I will be healed" (Mark 5:28). So in the church we confess our wounds. We want to be healed.

And you do want all to be healed, Lord, though all do not wish to be healed. You, Lord, say that you are sick, and you feel our infirmity in the least of us, saying: "I was sick and you looked after me" (Matthew 25:36).

When Peter excused himself from having you wash his feet, you said, "Unless I wash you, you have no part with me" (John 13:8).

So then what fellowship can anyone have with you, if they do not receive the keys of the kingdom of heaven?

Amen.

— *Ambrose of Milan*

BLESS THIS PEOPLE

God of compassion, I stretch out my hand upon your people and pray that the hand of truth may be stretched out and blessing given them on account of your lovingkindness.

May a hand of devotion, power, sound discipline, cleanness, and all holiness bless this people. Would you continually preserve them and help them grow through your only begotten Jesus Christ in the Holy Spirit, both now and to all the ages of the ages, amen.

— *Serapion Scholasticus*

GUARD YOUR PEOPLE, LORD

Lord God Almighty and true God, nothing compares to you.

You are everywhere, and present in all things, but you are not part of your creation.

You are not bound by place, and you do not grow old in time. You are not terminated by the ages. You are not deceived by words, and not created by anything.

You require no one to look after you, and you are above all corruption. You are free from change, and by nature you never vary.

You inhabit inaccessible light. You are invisible by nature, but are known to all thinking people who seek you with a good mind—your people who truly see and who have believed on Christ. You are the God of Israel.

Be gracious to me, and hear me, for the sake of your name.

Bless those who bow before you, and grant them the requests of their hearts, for their good. Do not reject any of them from your kingdom. Instead, set them apart for you. Guard, cover, and help them. Deliver them from the adversary, and from every enemy. Keep their houses and families safe, and guard them as they come and go.

For to you belongs the glory, praise, majesty, worship, and adoration, and to your Son Jesus, your Christ, our Lord and God and King, and to the Holy Spirit, now and always, forever and ever, amen.

— *Apostolic Constitutions*

PRAYER FOR PEACE FOR THE FLOCK

Without ceasing, my God, I will step into the doorway of your house, asking boldly for your grace, to receive it with confidence. Lord, our hope, be our wall.

If the earth gives life many times over to a grain of wheat, so will your grace enrich my prayers, even more. As you hear the voices of my people—their sighs and groans— open the doors of your mercy. For you were once a child, and you know what it was like.

Listen to the prayers of your children!

When sheep see the wolves, they flee to the shepherd for shelter under his staff. Your flock has seen the wolves, and they cry out in terror! Let your cross be a staff to drive away whatever would swallow them up.

Angels came down and proclaimed peace to the baby born in a cattle stall. I pray for the same peace, for my people— the peace that we could never find on our own. It took a baby, the son of Mary.

Have mercy, Lord who was once a child, on these children. Hear the cry of your little ones. Save them by your grace. They cry out from the midst of this flock of sheep to the shepherd of all.

Deliver us!

Amen.

— Ephraim the Syrian

Spare your people, Lord

Spare your people, O Lord, and do not allow your heritage
to be treated unfairly (Joel 2:17).

Feed us, Lord, so we do not become as we were in the
beginning, when you did not rule over us, and we did not
call on your name.

"We are objects of contempt to our neighbors, of scorn
and derision to those around us" (Psalm 79:4), because
wicked doctrines have come into your inheritance.
They have polluted your holy temple. The daughters of
strangers have rejoiced over our troubles.

A little while ago we were of one mind and one tongue, but
now we are divided into many tongues. But, Lord our God,
give us your peace, which we have lost by setting aside
your commandments.

We know none other than you, Lord. We call you by your
name.

"He … has made the two groups one and has destroyed
the barrier, the dividing wall of hostility" (Ephesians 2:14).
And the wall is the iniquity that has sprung up. So gather
us one by one, Lord, as your new Israel, building up
Jerusalem and gathering together the outcasts.

Let us be made one flock once more, all of us fed by you.
For you are the good shepherd who gives his life for his
sheep (John 10:11).

"Awake, Lord! Why do you sleep? Rouse yourself! Do not reject us forever" (Psalm 44:23).

Rebuke the winds and the sea. Give your church calm and safety from the waves.

Amen.

— Theodoret

EVERY CREATURE ADORES YOU

O God of our fathers and Lord of mercy, in your wisdom you formed humans as thinking creatures, and we are beloved by you more than all the other beings upon this earth. You gave us authority to rule over the creatures upon the earth.

You also ordained rulers for security of life, and leaders for regular worship.

Now would you also look down and make your face shine upon your people—those who bow the neck of their heart to you? Bless them by Christ, through whom you have opened up our minds to the Scriptures.

You have revealed yourself to us. Every thinking creature owes you their adoration, and to the Spirit, who is the Comforter, forever, amen.

— Apostolic Constitutions

PRESERVE THOSE YOU HAVE CALLED

Creator of all, preserve unbroken those you have called through your Son, Jesus Christ. He has called us from darkness to light, from ignorance to knowing the glory of his name.

Lord, our hope rests on your name, the creator of every living creature. You have opened the eyes of our heart to know you.

You behold the depths, and are eyewitness to everything we have done. You are the savior of those in despair. You help those in danger.

You are the creator and guardian of all, you multiply the nations of the earth, and you have chosen all who love you through Jesus Christ, your beloved Son.

We beg you, Lord and Master: be our help and encouragement.

Rescue those among us who are facing hard times. Have mercy on the lowly. Lift up the fallen. Show yourself to the needy. Heal the ungodly. Convert the wanderers among your people. Feed the hungry. Release our prisoners. Raise up the weak. Comfort the fainthearted.

Let all unbelievers know that you alone are God, that Jesus Christ is your Son, and that we are your people and the sheep of your pasture.

Amen.

— Clement of Rome

WE PRAY FOR THE CHURCH, FOR PEACE

Lord, we pray for peace in this world, and in our churches, spread around the world. God of the whole world, give us your everlasting peace, and take it not away.

Preserve us. Keep the church unshaken and free from the waves of this life, founded on a rock until the end of the age.

We pray for this local church, that the Lord of the whole world would preserve and keep it unshaken, and free from the waves of this life, until the end of the world. Stoop down to us here to keep us following the hope of heaven, as we rightly divide your word of truth.

We pray for our pastors and those in leadership. God of compassion, give them health and honor in godliness and right living. We pray for your protection and mercy in their lives.

We pray for those who give, that you would return to them eternal things for earthly things.

We pray for new believers, that you would strengthen and confirm them in their faith.

We pray for the sick, that you would deliver and heal them from every disease, and restore them to us in full health.

We pray for those who travel, and we pray for those in prison. We pray for those who oppose or even hate us, and for those who persecute us. Pacify their anger and scatter their wrath.

We pray for those who are still outside the fellowship, and for those who have wandered. Save them, Lord.

We pray for the youngest, that you would meet them and perfect them in holy reverence for you, and bring them to a complete age.

Preserve us by your grace to the end, and deliver us from the evil one. Keep us from scandals and preserve us for your kingdom. Raise us up by your mercy, as we dedicate ourselves to one another and to you, the living God, through Jesus Christ, amen.

— *Apostolic Constitutions*

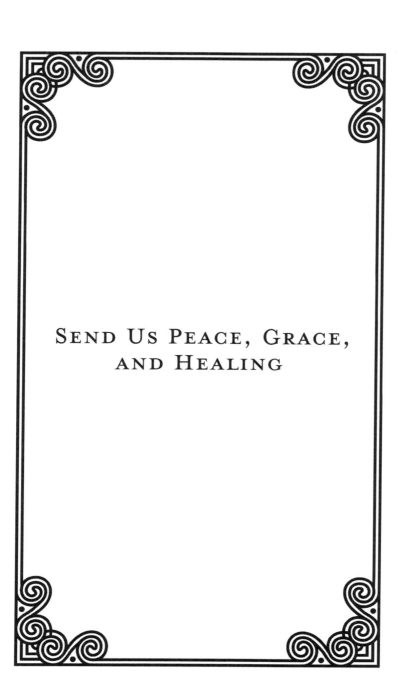

SEND US PEACE, GRACE, AND HEALING

OPEN THE SEA OF LOVE TO US

O God, who is the unsearchable abyss of peace, the indescribable sea of love, the fountain of blessings, and the source of affection—you send peace to those who receive it.

Open to us today your sea of love, and water us with abundant streams from the riches of your grace, and from the sweet springs of your kindness.

Make us children of quietness and heirs of peace.

Kindle in us the fire of your love. Sow in us reverence for you. Strengthen our weakness in your power.

Bind us close to you and to each other in one firm and unbreakable bond of unity.

Amen.

— *Clement of Rome*

POUR OUT YOUR PROMISE TO US, LORD

You have given your heart, O Lord, to your believers. You will never fail, nor will you ever be without fruits.

One hour of your faith is days and years. Who puts on your grace, and is hurt?

Your seal is known, your creatures know it, and your heavenly hosts possess it. Angels wear it.

You have given us your fellowship. It was not that you were in need of us, but that we are in need of you.

Distill your dew upon us and open your rich fountains that pour forth to us milk and honey.

For all was revealed before you as God, and ordered from the beginning before you. And you, O God, have made all things. Hallelujah!

Amen.

— Odes of Solomon

Show us your rainbow, Lord

Lord, you were gracious to Noah through your promise
and through your rainbow. You were gracious. If the
flood was going to destroy the earth, your rainbow
stretched over it, to banish the destruction and
encourage us once again.

As you have promised peace, so let your rainbow turn
away your wrath.

Show us your rainbow, stretched out against the flood.
Because, see! The waves of this flood are lapping against
our walls.

Noah sprinkled the blood of animal sacrifices, and that
worked for his family and future generations. How much
more powerful will be the blood of your only begotten
Son, that the sprinkling of his blood should hold back
our life's flood.

Be satisfied with the gift upon my altar, Lord, and save
me from this deadly flood. Both your signs will bring
deliverance. To Noah, your rainbow, and to me, your
cross. Your rainbow will hold back the flood of rain, and
your cross separates the waters.

Amen.

— *Ephraim the Syrian*

MAKE US HAPPY IN YOU

Lord my God, Lord *our* God, make us happy in you. We do not want to be happy in gold, silver, or real estate—not from earthly, vain, and transitory goods of this perishable life.

Do not let us speak with pride. Instead, make us happy in you, since we will never lose you. We are not lost with you. Happy are those whose God is the Lord. You will not be angry if we say that you are our estate—you are all we own—for we read that "you alone are my portion" (Psalm 16:5).

What a wonderful thing that we are your inheritance, and you are ours. And we do not detract from your honor to say that you cultivate us. Because if we cultivate you as our God, you cultivate us as your field. As the Lord said, "I am the vine; you are the branches." And, "My Father is the gardener" (John 15). So you do cultivate us. And if we yield fruit, you gather.

But if under the attention of so great a hand we are still barren, or we bring forth thorns instead of good fruit, I would be afraid to say what happens.

We turn to you, instead.

Amen.

— Augustine of Hippo

HOW YOU HAVE LOVED US!

How you have loved us, good Father! You who did not spare your only Son, but delivered him up for us, the ungodly.

How you have loved us! The one who was equal to you was made subject even to death on a cross. He alone had power to lay down his life, and power to take it up again.

For us he was both victor and victim—but victor in the end, *because* he was the victim.

For us he was both priest and sacrifice—but priest in the end, *because* of the sacrifice.

And so we were made children of God. And my hope is strong in you, that you will heal my infirmities by him who sits at your right hand, and who prays for us. Otherwise I would despair, because my infirmities are many and great.

But your medicine is greater.

We might imagine that your Word is far from us, and give up, unless he had been made flesh and dwelt among us.

Amen.

— *Augustine of Hippo*

YOU ARE ABLE TO PROVIDE

Like the eyes of a son to his father, O Lord, so are my eyes toward you at all times.

For with you are my consolations and my delight.

Do not turn your mercies from me, O Lord, and do not take away your kindness.

Stretch out to me your right hand at all times, and be my guide even to the end.

Let me be well-pleasing before you, because of your glory and your name. Preserve me from evil, and let your meekness abide with me, and the fruits of your love.

Teach me the psalms of your truth, that I may bring forth fruit in you. And open to me the harp of your Holy Spirit, that with all its notes I may praise you, O Lord.

Give to me according to the multitude of your tender mercies, and grant our prayers very soon. You are able to provide for all our needs. Hallelujah!

Amen.

— *Odes of Solomon*

YOUR POWER SUBDUES ALL

In my affliction I will call on the power that subdues all.
Lord, you are the power who is able to subdue the captor.
Glory to your grace!

God who is so good, you have repaid me with mercies that
you never borrowed from me. You have given me grace for
my misdeeds. Justice for my offenses. And your mercy has
covered over all my sins.

Send down your love, O Lord, and pour out your
righteous wrath. Your wrath to destroy, and your love to
rescue all the captives.

The evil one would have thrown me with a sling into
perdition, but you have bound up and kept my soul in the
bundle of life.

In the presence of so much grace, and the mercies that
surround me, how can I ever praise you enough?

Amen.

— *Ephraim the Syrian*

WORK FOR ME YOUR RESURRECTION

O my Lord, work for me your resurrection, not from your power to make things happen, but out of your love. Though your power could turn a sinner as well, work for me the resurrection that grows out of your mercy.

And even if your justice would not normally allow it, let there be an opening today for your grace. Remember that in your grace, I sought refuge.

Amen.

— *Ephraim the Syrian*

HEAL THOSE WHO ARE SICK, LORD

Lord, you have fashioned our bodies and our souls. You care for and govern the human race. Have mercy in your gentle love. We pray for your help and healing for those who are sick.

Rebuke the sicknesses, Lord. Raise up those who are lying down. Give glory to your holy name, and to your only begotten Jesus Christ, through whom to you is the glory and the strength in the Holy Spirit, both now and to all the ages of the ages, amen.

— *Serapion Scholasticus*

Receive us into your presence, Lord

Word of God, Light and Life, Wisdom and Might—I rejoice in all your names.

You who bear all things, binding them by the word of your power...

Receive this prayer as the completion of my offerings, a thanksgiving, and at the same time a humble request.

I pray that we may suffer no evil beyond those necessary and sacred cares in our life.

Keep us from the tyranny of the body and its illnesses. You see, O Lord, how it bows me down.

Keep us also from your own sentence, if we are to be condemned by you. If you would spare us (as we would ask), and be received into your presence, we will offer you acceptable sacrifices on your altar, to Father, Word, and Holy Spirit.

For to you belongs all glory and honor and might, world without end, amen.

— *Gregory Nazianzen*

SHOW US YOUR MAJESTY

It is enough, Almighty God, more than enough. Have we paid yet the consequences of arrogant wickedness? It is plain that those who have broken faith cannot be safe.

Turn again, O Lord, and set up the banners of your faith.

No military eagles lead our army, but it is your name, Lord Jesus, and your worship. Your majesty has long defended and rescued us.

Show us now a plain sign of your majesty.

Show us that anyone who believes you are the true Lord of hosts, the captain of the armies of heaven...

Anyone who believes you are the true power and wisdom of God, and not a created being, subject to time...

These are the people who may, upheld by the aid of your supreme might, win the prize of victory for their faith.

Amen.

— Ambrose of Milan

YOU PROVIDE OUR ENDLESS HOME

You are our hope, O God, and you provide our endless home. If we gain your pardon through our prayers and vigils, Lord, in your mercy—grant our requests.

Grant us, O Christ, to know your faultless designs. Gracious King, you give life to those who adore you. With the unbegotten Father, you are one majesty, on high.

Grant through the fellowship of the Comforter a triple support to aid us, so that crowds of worshipers may prolong your praise, without ceasing. It is right that we focus on keeping a vigil of worship before you. Even through the starry night we will see a light beyond candlelight, and we will trust in your light.

At your table you will end our solemn fasting. You who promise even more blessings, we praise you in unison. Ruler of all, give us poor mortals the power to express the power of the Almighty.

Your fountain cleanses the sinner, and we are made right through your new creation. You bring forgetfulness of sins, now laid aside. You cause your cleansed lambs to shine white as the snow. The hope and support of sinners, your word brings light—even as we would be washed clean in the Jordan and set apart for you.

The Sinless One was hurried to the cross—the most dreaded of penalties—that by his death he might renew the life we forfeited. Jesus, you yourself became the theme of praise for all your matchless deeds.

Who is worthy to express the praises of the Lord? Can human tongues enrich your renown, of which angel choirs echo above?

You opened your splendid palace for Stephen when he was stoned to death. You gave the keys of heaven to Peter, and much more—you added Paul the persecutor to your flock. So the one who urged on Stephen's killers became a teacher of the people, just as the thief on the cross who confessed your name received a place in paradise.

So you will graciously allow us, your servants of these latter days, to grow in grace, led by Peter's teaching. Give us a heart established with firm faith. And grant that I, when you lift me up, may join those who live again when you call the fellowship of the earth-born to heaven.

You are our hope, O God, and you provide our endless home! Amen.

— *Ausonius*

Whisper peace

Jesus, Deliverer, come to me. Soothe my voyaging over life's sea.

Then, when the storm of death roars as it sweeps by, whisper to me, O Truth of truth:

"Peace! It is I."

— *Anatolius of Constantinople*

Keep us, the descendants of Adam and Eve

O mighty Father of all things—earth, sea, air, and hell are all subject to you, and all the expanse of heaven emblazoned with the stars.

Those who are guilty tremble before you, while the blameless come before you with prayer and praise.

You reward our course through these few years and the swift close of our frail being with the prize of everlasting life. Keep us, the descendants of Adam and Eve.

Gracious Father, grant to the world your Word, who is your Son, and who is God, in all things like you and equal with you—very God of very God, living God of the source of life.

He, guided by your will, caused that Spirit which once moved over the face of the deep to bring our dullness to life with the cleansing waters of eternal life.

You are the object of our faith—three, yet one in source. Sure hope of our salvation!

Grant me pardon and bestow on me the gift of life I yearn for, if I embrace this diversity of persons, united in power, eternal Father, O Christ most merciful.

Amen.

— *Ausonius*

REDEEM ME FROM THAT OLD LIFE

In this beginning, O God, you have made heaven and earth—
through your Word, your Son, your power, your wisdom,
and your truth. All of them speak and create wonder.

Who can comprehend such things, and who can explain it?

What is it that shines through me and that strikes my heart
without injury, so that I shudder and burn? I shudder
because I am unlike it, and I burn because I am like it.

Wisdom itself shines through me, clearing away my fog
that would overwhelm me and make me faint in the
darkness and burden of my punishment.

For my strength is brought down in my need. I cannot
endure even my blessings, until you, Lord, heal my
infirmities. You have been gracious to me despite all my sins.

You will also redeem my life from corruption, and crown
me with your mercy and lovingkindness. You will satisfy
me with good things so my youth is renewed like the eagle's.

For we are saved by this hope, and we patiently await your
promises. I will cry out in confidence because of what is
written: "How many are your works, Lord! In wisdom
you made them all" (Psalm 104:24).

This wisdom is the beginning, and in that beginning you
made heaven and earth.

Amen.

— Augustine of Hippo

Hear me in your grace

Come to my rescue, one and only God.

You are the one true and eternal substance. In you there is no lack of agreement, no confusion, no shifting change, no poverty, and no death.

In you there is supreme harmony, supreme reason to believe, supreme steadfastness, supreme fullness—life supreme!

In you nothing is lacking, and nothing is redundant. The one who brings forth and the one who is brought forth are one.

By your laws the world spins, and stars show their courses in the sky. The sun lights up the day and the moon the night. All your framework—how light changes to night, how the moon waxes and wanes, how spring changes to summer and fall and winter in order ... all is maintained in your mighty constancy, month after month, cycle after cycle.

By your laws, Lord, our souls are free to choose. Reward or pain result. You provide all benefits and withhold all evils. Above you there is nothing. Beyond you there is nothing. Without you there is nothing.

Those who have come to know themselves make this discovery: you have made humanity in your image and likeness.

So hear me, Lord, hear me in your grace. My God, my
King, my Father, my Cause, my Hope, my Wealth, my
Honor, my House, my Country, my Health, my Light, my
Life.

Hear me, hear me in your grace—in that way that is
known to so few, but to those few known so well.

Amen.

— *Augustine of Hippo*

HELP US FLEE FROM VICE

Lord, as we are conscious of things present and future,
help us flee from vice, and strive after virtue, so that we
may not labor fruitlessly or randomly.

Instead, let us both enjoy the security here on earth, and
partake of the glory there in heaven—glory that you grant
for all of us, by the grace and love you grant in our Lord
Jesus Christ, to whom be the glory and might forever and
ever, amen.

— *John Chrysostom*

BRING US RAIN, LORD

Creator of heaven and earth, you who have crowned the
heavens through the choir of stars, you have honored the
earth with its fruits for our benefit. You have freely given
to your creation.

We pray now that you would grant us the rain we need.
Cause the ground to bear fruit and to produce abundance,
on account of your lovingkindness and goodness.

And remember those who call on you. Honor your church
and hear our prayers. Bless all the earth through your only
begotten Jesus Christ, through whom to you is the glory
and the strength in the Holy Spirit, both now and to all
the ages of the ages, amen.

— *Serapion Scholasticus*

PROTECT US, LORD

FOR HELP IN THE MIDST OF
PERSECUTION

There is a joy that is affliction, where misery is hidden. And in that new world there is a misery that is a fountain of joys.

Woes are hidden in the happiness my persecutor has gained, so I rejoice. Happiness is concealed in the wretchedness he handed me.

Who will not praise the one who gave us life, and can do it again? I see good news in the midst of evil.

Healer of all, you have visited me in my sicknesses. I cannot pay you for your medicines. They are priceless. And your mercies surpass your medicines. I cannot buy them; you give them freely. You barter them for tears.

Master, without mercy, and with its king far away, how can a lonely city stand against an approaching enemy? You are a harbor and a refuge at all times. When the seas covered me, your mercy came down and pulled me out.

So once again, lay hold of me! Let me see the passion of your help. Apply the medicine of your salvation to my affliction. You are a medicine to heal all.

My trouble is great, and I hurry to complain about the one who afflicts me. Let your mercy take away the bitterness from the cup that my sins filled to the brim.

I look around everywhere, and I weep that I am alone.
Even with friends and supporters, only one has delivered
me. You alone. People around me have scattered, Lord,
like chickens running from eagles, and they hide in a
secret place.

May your peace bring them back.

Amen.

— Ephraim the Syrian

Help me, you who need nothing

Come now to my aid, you who are the only eternal and
true God—Father, and Son, and Holy Spirit—without
any variableness or turning, without any needs or lack of
power, and without death.

You who always dwell in the highest brightness, you are
always totally steadfast, self-sufficient, and one.

With you there is no lack of good; you are always full of
every good, for eternity. You are Father, and Son, and
Holy Spirit.

Amen.

— Augustine of Hippo

SHOW US THE WAY ONWARD

Help us to hold fast, Lord, to the rudder of life. Guide our eyes away from the furious waves of lust. Guide our ears and tongues, lest the one receive anything harmful, or the other speak what should never be said.

Do not let the tempest of passion overwhelm us, or the blows of depression beat us down, or the weight of sorrow drown us in its depths. Our feelings are waves. Help us to rise above them, steering a safe course through life. Otherwise, with life's dangers all around, our boats could tip and sink in the deep sea of sin.

Those at sea lift their eyes to heaven for guidance, and for the right course—by day following the sun, by night, following the Big Dipper, or the ever-shining stars. Help us also, as the psalmist said, to "lift up my eyes to you, to you who sit enthroned in heaven" (Psalm 123:1).

Help us to keep our eyes on the sun of righteousness, directed by your commands, as by some bright constellations. Do not let our eyes sleep, that the guidance of your commands would never cease.

"Your word is a lamp for my feet, a light on my path" (Psalm 119:105).

Help us to never fall asleep at our steering wheel. As long as we live, and amid the unstable circumstances of this world, Spirit, help and show us the way onward. Move us on by gentle winds of peace, until we one day arrive

safe and sound at the calm and waveless haven of God, to
whom be glory and majesty forever and ever, amen.

— Basil of Caesarea

THE WAR BEING WAGED AGAINST US

Lord God—you cheered David's heart during his worst
troubles. You gave power to Daniel even against the lions.
You made the children of Abraham victorious. Without
you, not even a little sparrow falls.

Now, Lord, take note of the war being waged against
us. You know how weak we are, by nature. The enemy is
trying to separate your workmanship from your glory. But
look upon us with compassion. Keep the lamp of your
commandments shining brightly within us, against all
attempts to extinguish it.

And by your light guide our paths. In your mercy allow us
to enjoy the happiness that is in you. For you are blessed
forever, world without end, amen.

— Shamuna the Martyr

Keep me until that day, Lord

Son of the all-highest Father, bringer of salvation, you to
whom your Begetter has freely committed all the powers
of his fatherhood, keeping none back in envy ... open a
way for these my prayers and safely waft them to your
Father's ears.

Grant me a heart, O Father, to hold out against all wrong
deeds, and deliver me from the serpent's deadly venom,
sin. Let it be enough that the serpent tricked our mother
Eve and involved Adam also in his deceit.

As their late-born descendants once foretold by prophets,
let us escape the snares which the death-dealing serpent
weaves.

Prepare a road that I, being freed from the fetters of this
frail body, may be led up on high—to the place where
in the clear heaven the Milky Way stretches above the
wandering clouds of the moon, on that road by which the
holy ones of old departed from the earth. Show me the
path which Elijah, caught up in the chariot, once made his
way alive above our lower air, and also Enoch, who went
before his end without change of body.

Grant me, O Father, the everlasting light for which I yearn.
I will swear not by gods of stone. Instead, I look up to one
altar of awful sacrifice alone, and I bring there the offering
of a stainless life—because I recognize you as Father of the
Only-Begotten, our Lord and God. And, joined with both,
the Spirit who brooded over the face of the waters.

Grant me your pardon, Father, and relieve my anguish.
May no crime bring me to ruin, nor suspicion tarnish my
name. (Small difference there seems between the real and
supposed guilt.) Keep from me the means to do ill, and let
me ever have the calm power to do well.

Let me be moderate in food and dress, dear to my friends,
and ever careful to do nothing to shame your name. In
mind and body let me be free from pain, and let all my
limbs perform their functions.

Let me enjoy peace and live quietly, counting as nothing
all that astounds on earth.

And when the hour of my last day is come, grant that the
conscience of a life well spent will not cause me to fear
death, nor long for it. When, through your mercy, I am
cleansed from my secret faults, let me despise all else, and
let my one delight be to await in hope your judgment.

And if that season tarries and the day delays, keep me
far from that fierce tempter, the serpent, with his false
attractions.

These prayers of a devoted soul, although I tremble, I
claim before the eternal Father, and Son of God, Savior,
God and Lord. You are Glory, Word, and Son. You are
very God of very God and Light of Light, who remains
with the eternal Father, reigning throughout all ages, and
whose praise the songs of David echo forth until voices fill
the air with their "Amen."

— *Ausonius*

YOU ARE THE GARLAND ON MY HEAD

I will give thanks to you, O Lord, because I love you.

O Most High, you will not forsake me, for you are my hope.

Freely I have received your grace, and I will live by it.

My persecutors will come and not see me. A cloud of darkness will fall on their eyes, and an air of thick gloom will darken them. They will have no light to see, and they may not take hold of me.

For my hope is in the Lord, and I will not fear. Because you are my salvation, I will not fear. You are a garland on my head and I will not be moved. Even if everything should be shaken, I stand firm.

And if all things visible should perish, I will not die, because you are with me, Lord, and I am with you. Hallelujah!

Amen.

— *Odes of Solomon*

Help Us to Be
More like Jesus

BE GRACIOUS TO US

Be gracious, O Instructor, to us your children. You are
our Father, the chariot driver of Israel, Son and Father,
both in one.

To those of us who obey your ways, grant that we may
look more and more like you. With all that is in us, may
we know you as our good God, not as a harsh judge.

For us who know your peace, who have been brought into
your kingdom, and who have sailed through the storms
of sin, bring us into calm waters by your Holy Spirit
and your indescribable wisdom, by night and day, to the
perfect day.

May we give thanks and praise alone to the Father and the
Son, the Son and the Father, the Son who is our instructor
and teacher, with the Holy Spirit, all in one, in whom is all,
and for whom all is one.

Eternity is yours, and it radiates your glory. We belong to
you, the all-good, all-lovely, all-wise, all-just one. To you
be glory now and forever, amen.

— *Clement of Alexandria*

HELP US LOVE ONE ANOTHER

Lord, help us never to distance ourselves from you.
Instead, let us hold tightly to the care of our souls, and to
love each other.

Let us not injure other members of our own body, as that
would be insane. But let us be kind to others even more as
we see them feeling poorly.

Though we often see many persons physically suffering
from difficult or incurable illness, we never stop offering
possible remedies. What is worse than painful arthritis in
the foot or hand? Would we just cut off the limbs?

Not at all! We do everything possible to relieve the pain,
even if we cannot cure the disease.

Let us do the same for our brothers and sisters in Christ.
Even if they have an incurable disease, help us to still tend
to them, and let us bear one another's burdens.

That way, we fulfill the law of Christ, and obtain
the promised good things, through the grace and
lovingkindness of our Lord Jesus Christ, to whom be
glory forever and ever with the Father and the Holy Spirit,
amen.

—John Chrysostom

We will keep knocking on your door

Lord, I have your testimony in writing that says, "Have I any pleasure at all that the wicked should die ... and not that he should return from his ways, and live?" (Ezekiel 18:23). It was for this that you came down: to save sinners, to raise the dead, to bring the lost to life, and to give light to those in darkness.

In truth you came, and called us to adoption as your children, to a holy city which is ever at peace, to the life that never dies, to glory incorruptible. Only let us put a good finish to our beginning.

Let us abide in poverty, as strangers, suffering affliction. Let us knock with persistence on your door.

Near as the body is to the soul, you are nearer. You come and open the locked doors of the heart and shower us with the riches of heaven. You are good and kind to us, and your promises cannot lie, if only we continue seeking you to the end.

Glory be to the compassions of the Father and of the Son and of the Holy Spirit forever.

Amen.

— *Pseudo-Macarius*

CLOTHE US WITH FIRE, LORD

Lord, let us stretch our mind toward heaven—and let us
be held fast by that desire. Let us clothe ourselves with
spiritual fire, and let us be equipped with its flame.

No one who bears the flame fears wild beasts, or other
people, or any kind of snare. As long as we are armed with
fire, all things stand out of our way. All things pull back.

No one can tolerate the flame. It cannot be endured; it
consumes all.

So let us clothe ourselves with this fire, Lord. Let us offer
up glory to our Lord Jesus Christ, to whom be glory,
might, and honor with the Father and the Holy Spirit, now
and forever, world without end, amen. Thanks be to God!

—*John Chrysostom*

STRETCH YOUR WINGS OVER US

Lord, you alone lack pride, because you are the only
true Lord, who has no lord. Have I also lost this kind of
temptation, or can I avoid it my whole life? Do I wish for
the respect and love of others, and for no other reason
than to receive a joy that contains no joy?

What a miserable life and a foul boastfulness! People neither
fear you nor love you purely. You resist the proud and give
grace to the humble. You thunder down on the world's
ambitions, and the foundations of the mountains tremble.

Because our culture deems it necessary to be loved and
respected by others, our adversary comes hard at us,
spreading his snares everywhere of "well done, well done!"
And by grasping at those snares in greed, we can be taken
unaware. We can sever our joy from your truth, attach that
joy to human deception, and so be pleased at being loved
and respected—not for your sake, but *instead* of you.

In this way we would follow our enemy, the one who set
up a throne in the north. We would become like him, not
in love, but in the bonds of punishment. Dark and chilled,
we would serve the one who perversely and crookedly
imitates you.

If we were praised for some gift you had given us, and
we rejoiced more about the praise for ourselves than that
we actually had a gift from you, we might be praised, but
not by you. Even if the person who complimented us
took pleasure in the gift of God itself, we would be more

pleased with the human gift, the human praise, rather than God's gift.

But see, Lord, we are your little flock. Take ownership of us as your own. Stretch your wings over us, and let us fly beneath them. Be our glory, let us be loved for you, and let us fear your word in us.

Amen.

—*Augustine of Hippo*

HELP US TO LEAVE BEHIND OUR WORRIES

Lord, help us to leave behind our worries about what everyone around us thinks of us—whether it is about their insults ... or their honors.

Instead, let us be diligent about one thing only: that we harbor no evil thing, nothing that displeases you, nor insult even ourselves.

That way, we will enjoy much glory both in this life and, as God grants, in the world to come.

By the grace and love toward us of our Lord Jesus Christ, to whom be glory, world without end, amen.

—*John Chrysostom*

WE PRAY FROM GENESIS TO REVELATION

Lord my God, hear my prayer. Let your mercy respond to
my desires. I am not anxious for myself alone, but also for
the sake of love. You see my heart, and so it is.

I will sacrifice to you the service of my thoughts and my
words. Do give me what I may offer back to you. For I am
poor and needy, and you are rich to all who call upon you.
You care for us.

Separate from my inward and outward lips all rashness
and lying. Let Scripture be my pure delight. Do not let
me be deceived in the written words, nor let me deceive
others with them.

Hear us and show pity, Lord, light of the blind and
strength of the weak. You are also the light of those that
see, and strength of the strong.

Hear my soul cry out of the deep. If you could not hear us
there, where should we go? Where would we cry?

The day is yours. The night is yours. The moments fly by at
your command. So grant us a space for our meditations on
the hidden things of your law, and do not close the door
to those of us who knock. You would not have written so
many deep secrets in Scripture for nothing, just as you did
not create deer to roam the forest for nothing.

Perfect me, Lord, and reveal your deep truths. See? Your
voice is my joy. Your voice far surpasses the greatest
pleasures. Give what I love, for I do love, and you have

given. Do not forget your gifts or turn away from a thirsty green plant.

Let me confess to you whatever I find in your book, and hear the voice of praise. Then I will drink you in as I meditate on your law, right from the beginning, where you made heaven and earth, all the way to the everlasting reign with you in your holy city, amen.

— *Augustine of Hippo*

RESTRAIN OUR THOUGHTS

Restrain our thoughts, O Lord and God, so they do not wander amid the vanities of this world.

Grant that I may be united to the affection of your love, though I am unworthy.

Sow in me the good seed of humility. Through your mercy, hide me under the wings of your grace. Because if you kept track of sin, Lord, who could stand?

There is mercy with you.

Amen.

— *Adæus and Maris*

FOR GIFTS LIKE STARS

Lord, I beg you—let truth spring from the earth, and let
righteousness look down from heaven. And let there be
lights in the sky.

Let us share our food with the hungry, and bring the
homeless to our homes. Let us clothe the naked, and never
despise those who do not look like us.

Whatever good has sprung from the earth, we will call good.
May our temporary light break forth. And from where we
stand, blessed as we are to think on you and obtain the
Word of Life from above, let us shine as lights in the world,
holding fast to the starry ceiling of your Scripture.

In the secret of your judgment, as before the world was
made, you separated light and darkness. So now that
your grace is spread around the world, let your spiritual
children discern also between light and darkness, and the
signs of the times.

Now that the night is far spent, and the day is at hand,
crown the year with blessings. Send the laborers of your
goodness into your harvest. Some have sown, others have
labored, and you send us into another field whose harvest
is ready.

In this way you grant the prayers of those who ask, and
you bless the years of the just. You are the same, and in
your time you prepare a crown for our passing years.

In your time you bestow heavenly blessings on the earth.
To one by the Spirit you give a word of wisdom. To
another you give faith, and to yet another a gift of the light
of the clearest truth, for the rule of the day.

By the same Spirit you give the word of knowledge, the gift
of healing, or the working of miracles. To others, prophecy,
the discerning of spirits, or different tongues.

And all these gifts are like stars. They all result from one
and the same Spirit, given to each as you decide, Lord, as
you cause the stars to shine, to benefit all.

All-wise God, speak to us in your book—your sky—so we
may discern all things, in signs, in times, days, and years.

Amen.

— *Augustine of Hippo*

LET ME ALWAYS SEEK YOUR FACE

O Lord our God, we believe in you—the Father and the Son and the Holy Spirit. Because Truth would not say, Go, baptize all nations in the name of the Father and of the Son and of the Holy Spirit, unless you were a Trinity.

You would not command us to be baptized in the name of one who is not the Lord God himself. Nor would you have said, "Hear, O Israel, the Lord your God is one God," unless you were so much a Trinity as to be one Lord God.

If you, O God, were yourself the Father, and were yourself the Son, your Word Jesus Christ, and the Holy Spirit your gift, we would not read in the book of truth, "God sent his Son."

Nor would you, only-begotten one, say of the Holy Spirit, "whom the Father will send in my name," and "whom I will send to you from the Father."

As I step out by this rule of faith, I have sought you so far as I have been able, and so far as you have made me able. I have wanted to see with my understanding what I believed. I have argued and labored much.

O Lord my God, my one hope, please hear me, so that in my weariness I would not give up seeking you. Let me always ardently seek your face.

Give me strength to seek, you who have enabled me to find you, and have given me the hope of finding you more

and more. You see my strength and my illness; preserve
the one and heal the other.

You see my knowledge and my ignorance. Where you have
opened the door to me, receive me as I enter. Where you
have closed the door, open to me as I knock.

May I remember you, understand you, and love you.
Increase these things in me, until you have completely
renewed me.

Amen.

— Augustine of Hippo

Give me a pure heart

O God Almighty, Father of Jesus Christ, your only Son—give
me an undefiled body, a pure heart, and a watchful mind.

Help me to know the truth at all times, under the influence
of the Holy Spirit, who will bring me to the truth and help
me to enjoy it in the assurance you give me.

I ask this through Christ, by whom all glory belongs to
you in the Holy Spirit forever, amen.

— Apostolic Constitutions

WE WILL LOVE YOU WITH OUR WHOLE HEART

If you came upon the earth and took such care of perishable bodies, how much more will you care for the immortal soul, made after your own likeness?

It is because of our unbelief and our divided mind that we have not yet found the spiritual cure. It is because we do not love you with all our heart, or that we really do not believe you.

Let us then believe, and come to you in reality, so that you may speedily work the true cure in us. You have promised to give the Holy Spirit to those who ask, and to open to those who knock, and to be found by those who seek.

And the one who has made the promise cannot lie. To you be glory and might for ever. Amen.

— *Pseudo-Macarius*

HELP US TO SHINE AND REST WITH YOU

Lord, you prayed, "I have come to bring fire on the earth, and how I wish it were already kindled!" (Luke 12:49).

This fire drives away devils and destroys sin. It is resurrection power and eternal life. It illuminates souls and strengthens our minds.

We pray that this fire may reach us also, that we would always walk in light, and never for a moment dash our feet against a stone (Psalm 91:12) but that we would shine as lights in the world and hold forth the word of everlasting life (Philippians 2:15).

As we enjoy ourselves among the good things of God, we pray also that we may rest with you in life, glorifying the Father, Son, and Holy Spirit, to whom be glory forever. Amen.

— *Pseudo-Macarius*

Help us find humility

Lord, you have said that David was a man after your own heart. Help us to gain the same kind of spirit as David, so that we may bear easily whatever suffering we face, and reap in this world the benefits of humility.

"Learn from me," you said, "for I am gentle and humble in heart, and you will find rest for your souls" (Matthew 11:29).

So that we may enjoy rest both here and hereafter, help us to diligently implant in our souls the mother of all things that are good—humility. With it, Lord, we can pass over the sea of this life without waves, and finally end our voyage in that calm harbor, by the grace and love toward others of our Lord Jesus Christ.

To you be glory and might forever and ever, amen.

—*John Chrysostom*

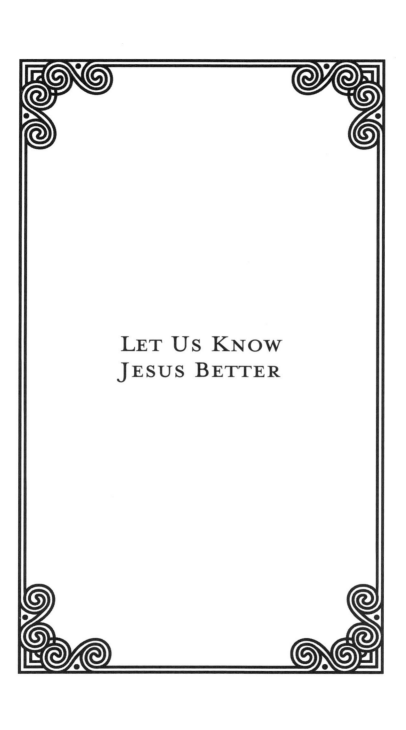

LET US KNOW
JESUS BETTER

LET ME SEE YOUR FACE

Lord, may I rest in you! If you would just enter my heart, and take it over completely, so I will forget all my troubles, and embrace you, my only good.

What do you mean to me? In your pity, teach me to say it.

Or what am I to you, that you demand my love? And if I do not give it, you are indignant, and I face grief? Is it then only a small sin to not love you?

Oh! For the sake of your mercy, Lord my God, tell me just what you are to me. Say to my soul: I am your salvation. Speak, that I may hear.

See, Lord, my heart is before you. Open its ears, and say to my soul:

I am your salvation.

After that, let me hurry to take hold of you. Do not hide your face from me. Let me die—lest I die—only let me see your face.

Amen.

—Augustine of Hippo

I WILL GROW INTO YOU, LORD

O Truth who is eternity, and Love who is the truth, and
Eternity who is love!

You are my God, and I sigh to you night and day. When
I first came to know you, you lifted me up to see—and
showed me that I still did not see.

You beat back the weakness of my sight, streaming your
strong beams of light over me, and I trembled with love
and awe. I could tell I was far from you, in a place where I
was very much unlike you.

It was as if I heard your voice, telling me:

"I am the food of those who have grown up. Grow, and I
will be your nourishment. You will not change me, but
you will be converted into me."

Amen.

— *Augustine of Hippo*

HELP ME TO FIND REAL LIFE

Lord, when I cling to you with all my being, my life will be a real life, wholly full of you.

But now since the one you fill is the one you must lift up, I am still a burden to myself. I am not yet full of you.

Joys of sorrow compete with sorrows of joy. On which side is the victory? I am not sure. Have pity on me, Lord! I am in trouble!

I do not hide my wounds. You are the physician; I am the sick.

You are the merciful; I am the miserable.

Isn't life on earth full of temptations? Who actually wishes for troubles and difficulties? You command that we endure difficulties but not love them. And even if we rejoice to endure, we would rather not have anything to endure.

In adversity, I desire to prosper. When I prosper, I fear adversity. Where is that middle place between the two, where life is not a temptation?

— *Augustine of Hippo*

KINDLE US AND DRAW US CLOSE

O my God, with thanksgiving allow me to confess to you your mercies.

Let my bones be covered with your love, like dew, and let them ask you:

"Who is like you, Lord?"

You have shattered my bonds, and I will offer to you a sacrifice of thanksgiving. I will explain to everyone just how you broke those bonds. And when they hear, they will say:

"Blessed be the Lord, in heaven and on earth. His name is wonderful!"

Stir us up, Lord. Kindle us and draw us close. Inflame us and grow sweet to us. Let us love, and let us run.

Amen.

— *Augustine of Hippo*

NOW MY SOUL IS FREE

Lord, I am your servant. You have shattered my bonds,
and I will offer to you the sacrifice of praise. Let my heart
and my tongue praise you. Let all my bones say, "O Lord,
who is like you?"

Then may you answer, "I am your salvation."

Who am I, and what am I? My deeds have been evil. Or if
not my deeds, then my words. And if not my words, then
my intentions.

But you, O Lord, are good and merciful. Your right hand
found out the depth of my death, and emptied the abyss of
corruption from the bottom of my heart. And your gift to
me was to nullify what I willed, and to will what you willed.

So from all of these years, and out of the lowest and
deepest place, my free will was called forth in a moment.
Then I could place my neck into your easy yoke, and place
my shoulders beneath your light burden.

Christ Jesus, you are my helper and redeemer!

All at once it was sweetness to me, and I wanted the
sweetness of that toy—your yoke. And what I was afraid
to be parted from was now a joy to be rid of. You threw
it all away for me, you who are the true and highest
sweetness. You threw it all away, and took its place. And it
became sweeter than all pleasure, though not to flesh and
blood. You were brighter than all light, but more hidden

than all depths. Higher than all honor, though not to those who are high in their own conceits.

Now my soul is free from the bitter cares of getting more things, and wallowing in filth, and scratching off the itch of lust. And my infant tongue speaks freely to you, my brightness, my riches, my health—the Lord my God.

Amen.

— *Augustine of Hippo*

I LOVE YOU ABOVE ALL ELSE

Lord, I love you above all other things.

You are the one I seek. You are the one I follow. You are the one I am ready to serve. I want to dwell under your rule, for you alone reign.

Command me as you will, but heal and open my eyes to see your wonders. And drive all foolishness and pride from me. Give me wisdom to understand you, and teach me where to look to see you.

Then I will gladly do what you command.

Amen.

— *Augustine of Hippo*

I HEARD YOUR VOICE BEHIND ME

Lord, let the light and the truth speak to me—not my own darkness.

I fell off into that, and became darkened. But even from that time, even from that time, I loved you.

I went astray, and remembered you. I heard your voice behind me, calling me to return. And I scarcely heard it, through the noise and confusion of the enemies of peace.

And now, see? I return in distress, panting in thirst for your fountain. Let no one stop me!

I will drink from your fountain, and so live. Do not let me be my own life. I did not know how to live. I was death to myself, and I revive in you.

Speak to me; speak with me. I have believed your word, and its words are full of mystery.

Amen.

—*Augustine of Hippo*

YOU ARE THE SOURCE

I call upon you, my God, my mercy and my creator. You forget me not, even when I forget you.

I call you into my soul, which you prepare for yourself through the longing you inspire in me.

Do not turn away from me now as I call upon you. You have drawn me with so many different and repeated calls, so I would hear you from afar, and call on the one who called me, and be saved.

For you, Lord, wiped away all my evil deservings, and you did not repay into my own hands—hands that had let you go. You prevented what should have happened from happening.

But in your goodness I am the work of your hands. Before I was, you were. You do not need me, and I am not good enough to be truly helpful to you, serving you. Your power would be no less if you lacked my service. Your land would not remain uncultivated without me.

But as I serve and worship you, I receive my wellbeing— from you. You are the source.

Amen.

— Augustine of Hippo

TEACH ME TO COME CLOSER TO YOU

How wonderful is your goodness, Lord, and so unlike all other good things.

I want to come to you. All I need on the way I desire from you. Without it, I cannot come to you.

If you turn away from me, I will perish. But I also know that you will not turn away from me unless I turn away from you. And I will not turn away from you, for you are the highest good.

No one who rightly seeks you does not find you. And the only way to rightly seek you is by your teaching. You teach us to seek you rightly, and how to seek you.

Good Father, free me entirely from the error in which I have wandered, and in which I still wander. Teach me instead the way to avoid every enemy on the way to you.

If I love no one above you, I ask that I may find you. And if I desire anything beyond measure and wrongly, deliver me from it. Make me worthy to behold you.

Amen.

— *Augustine of Hippo*

CONVERT ME WHOLLY TO YOU

Most ancient and wise Father, I commit my body to you, to keep it whole.

Yet I do not really know what I ask—whether I am asking for something useful or useless to me or to the friends I love and who love me.

Nor do I know how long you would keep my body whole. So I commit it to you, because you know better what I need.

I pray that you would always teach me, while I am in this body and this world. Help me always to speak with words that please you, and in ways that are best and most righteous in this life.

But above all else I earnestly pray that you would convert me wholly to you, and let nothing overcome me on this way, or prevent me from coming closer to you. Cleanse me while I am in this world, and make me humble. Give me loftiness of soul. Make me reasonable, just, and prudent, lacking nothing in your sight.

Help me both to recognize and love your wisdom, and in the end make me worthy to dwell in your blessed kingdom.

Amen.

— *Augustine of Hippo*

GUIDE US AND FEED US

GUIDE US, SHEPHERD OF THE SHEEP

You are the bridle of untamed colts, Lord, the wing of
unwandering birds.

You are the sure guide of babes and the shepherd of royal
lambs. Gather your simple children to praise you with
holy praise, to sing your songs with innocent mouths.

Christ, you are the guide of children.

O King of saints, all-powerful Word of the most high
Father, ruler of wisdom, support of sorrows and grief,
you are Lord throughout the ages, Jesus, Savior of the
human race.

You are the shepherd and caretaker, the rudder to steer
our course and the bridle to keep us from straying, the
heavenly wing of your all-holy flock.

You are the fisher of those whom you save and bring to life,
pulling in the fish who seek you from the hateful wave in a
sea of sin. You offer sweet life, instead.

Guide us, shepherd of the sheep. Gift us with reason,
guide us as children, unharmed.

O holy King, footsteps of Christ, the heavenly way, Word
without end. Age unending, eternal light, fount of mercy,
send us your righteousness. Glorious and honorable is the
life of those who sing praises to God.

O Christ Jesus, nourish us with heavenly milk, given by your wisdom. We are babes with tender mouths. Let us together sing simple praises, true hymns to Christ our King, in grateful offering for the teaching of life.

We sing in our simple way to you, the God of peace. Amen.

— *Clement of Alexandria*

FILL US, TRIUNE GOD

Blessed God, you who have fed me from my youth, and who gives food to all who live, fill our hearts with joy and gladness.

In that way, we will be fully equipped to abound unto every good work in Christ Jesus our Lord, with whom be unto you glory, honor, and might, with the Holy Spirit, forever.

Glory to you, O Lord! Glory to you, O Holy One! And glory to you, O King! You have given us meat to make us glad. Fill us with the Holy Spirit, that we may be found well-pleasing before you, and not ashamed when you give to everyone according to their works.

Amen.

— *John Chrysostom*

I PRESENT TO YOU A VICTORY GARLAND

Teacher, I present to you a victory garland for your head, woven of words picked from that spotless meadow where you feed your flocks, like the skilled worker bee, gathering its treasure from many a flower, that it may present its master a delicious offering.

Though but the least, I am still your servant. It is right for me to praise you for your commands.

O King, you are the great giver of good gifts to us all, and Lord of the good. You are our Father and maker of all. By your word you made heaven and everything in it. You brought forth sunshine and the day. You appointed the courses of the stars, showed the earth and sea their places.

You decided when the seasons should come in their circling courses, winter and summer, autumn and spring.

You created this ordered sphere out of a confused heap, and adorned the universe from a shapeless mass.

Grant to me life—a life well spent, always enjoying your grace. Help me to act and speak in all things as your Holy Scriptures teach.

May I ever praise you, and praise your co-eternal Word, who proceeds from you.

And give me neither poverty nor wealth, but only what is right, Father, in life—and then life's happy close, amen.

— *Clement of Alexandria*

FILL US WITH RIGHTEOUSNESS

Feed us, the children, as you would feed your sheep. Fill us with righteousness, Master. This is your own pasture. Feed us on your holy mountain, which is the church— towering high above the clouds, touching heaven.

"I will be your shepherd," you say. You will be near us, as a garment is close to the skin. You save us by covering us in the robe of immortality. You have anointed my body.

"They will call me," you say, "and I will say, 'Here am I.'"

You heard me sooner than I expected, my Master.

"And if you pass over," you say to me, "you will not fall."

For we who are passing over to immortality will not fall into corruption, because you will sustain us. So you have said, and so you have willed. That is the way you are, our Instructor, and you are righteously good.

Amen.

— *Clement of Alexandria*

GIVE ME REST BEHIND THE HAVEN OF MY WALLS

Lord, you see how the sea billows of life rise against me. It was easier for those in the ark—they only had to deal with a flood of water. Life's mounds and weapons and waves surround me.

The ark was a storehouse of natural treasures, while I am a storehouse of debts.

Your love subdued the waves around the ark. But I am left desolate against all the weapons of life that come against me.

The ark survived floodwaters, while the river of life still threatens me. The flood of life still threatens and dashes against my walls.

So may your all-sustaining power uphold my walls. They will not fall like the house that was built on the sand (Matthew 7), because I have not built my beliefs on the sand. My foundation is a rock; I have built my faith upon your rock. The secret foundation of my trust will support my walls.

The walls of Jericho fell because the people of that city had built their trust on sand. Moses built a wall in the sea, and his understanding was built on a rock. The foundation of Noah was on a rock, as well, supporting their wooden home in the sea.

O helmsman of that ark, be my pilot on dry land. You gave
the ark rest in the haven of the mountaintop. Give me rest,
as well, behind the haven of my walls.

Amen.

— *Ephraim the Syrian*

YOU ARE THE SWEET LIGHT OF MY HIDDEN EYES

Ruler of your creatures, how do you teach us those things
that are in the future? For you have taught your prophets.

How do you, to whom nothing is future, teach us about
future things? Or rather, how do you teach about future
things, as if they were in the present? For what does not
exist certainly cannot be taught as if it already exists.

This is too far away from what I can see. It is too mighty
for me. I cannot grasp it.

But by you I will be enabled when you have granted me
that privilege. You are the sweet light of my hidden eyes.

Amen.

— *Augustine of Hippo*

SHOW US HOW TO SEEK
FIRST THE KINGDOM

SWEEP AWAY THE LOVE OF MONEY

Lord, may love of money be put away in our conversation.
Money has been the lord over our freedom!

Let this money disease be swept away from us. Take away
the wealth that is so familiar and pleasant to us. Abolish
the root of that pleasure, and the customs and attitudes
that turn out to be so full of harm.

Evil things have possessed us through such customs. Cut
away that evil in our life, and take away the wealth that
distracts us in our church. Instead, let the church collect
souls, and in marvelous measure!

And let us not bury our dead without hope, or with
wailing and laments, like the world does. We bless you
who turns our bodies back to dust!

So now let good things possess us through new customs
that spring from you. Be the root and the cause of our help,
O Lord! And blessed be the Father who chose you, Jesus,
to give us new purpose in life.

Amen.

— *Ephraim the Syrian*

LORD, DECORATE OUR HOMES WITH YOUR GOODNESS

Lord, we want to invite you to our homes. So we decorate them with giving to the needy, with prayers, with requests, and with vigils that focus unceasingly on the needs of others. These are the decorations of Christ the King.

We are not ashamed then of having a humble house, if it has this kind of furniture.

But the decorations that come from unstoppable greed are the enemy of Christ. May those of us who are rich not pride ourselves on having an expensive house. Rather let us hide our faces, turn away from greed, and seek the other kind of decoration.

In so doing let us receive Christ in this life on earth, and there enjoy the eternal home, by the grace and love you have for us in Jesus Christ, to whom be glory and might, world without end, amen.

— John Chrysostom

WE CELEBRATE HOPE

Eternal Savior and King of all, you alone are mighty. You alone are the Lord, the God of all beings, and the God of our fathers, and of those before us—the God of Abraham, Isaac, and Jacob.

You are merciful and compassionate, long-suffering, and abundant in mercy. Every heart is open before you, every heart seen, every secret thought revealed.

To you the souls of the righteous cry aloud; upon you the hopes of the godly rest. You are Father of the blameless— and you hear the requests of those who call upon you with uprightness.

You know the unspoken prayers, for your providence reaches as far as our inmost parts. By your knowledge you search the thoughts of everyone. You search and know every region of the whole earth where the incense of prayer rises up to you.

Though this present world stands against your righteousness, you have opened the gate of mercy to everyone.

By giving us knowledge and natural judgment, and through your law, you show us how being rich is not forever, nor is the ornament of beauty. You prove to us how our strength and force are easily dissolved, and how all is vapor and vanity.

Only a good conscience of sincere faith passes through the midst of the heavens, returns with truth, and takes hold of the right hand of the joy to come.

So before the promise of the restoration of all things is even accomplished, the soul itself celebrates in joyful hope.

Amen.

— Apostolic Constitutions

HELP US TO IMITATE THE BEST

Lord, let us pattern our lives only on those things that are worthy of being imitated. Not gorgeous buildings or expensive estates, but on those people who have confidence in you.

Help us to imitate those who have riches in heaven—the owners of those treasures that make them truly rich.

Help us to imitate those who are poor for Christ's sake, so that we may attain the good things of eternity by the grace and love toward man of our Lord Jesus Christ.

Glory, might, and honor be unto him with the Father, together with the Holy Spirit, now and always, world without end, amen.

— John Chrysostom

HELP US FLY FROM GREED

Lord, help us to put aside the things of this world, in favor of the good things to come. This way, we will obtain both, by your grace.

Let us escape the bonds of worldly deceit, so that we may never fall into those things which would deliver us over to the unquenchable fire. We know that anyone who is a slave to money is held by its chains, both in the present and in the future. But those who escape this desire will gain freedom.

Redeemer of our souls, we ask that you would break apart our bonds and take away the cruel jailer. Having set us free from the burden of those iron chains, you would make our spirits lighter than any wing.

And as we pray to you, help us also to do our part. Help us to be serious about this in every way, so that we will be more quickly free of this evil that weighs us down, and see clearly our earlier condition, and then lay hold of the liberty which belongs to us, in your grace.

We want to be free, Lord. Help us to break into pieces the oppressive harness of greed, and by your grace gain wings toward heaven, through our Lord Jesus Christ, amen.

— *John Chrysostom*

LOOSE THE BONDS OF GREED

Lord, nothing, nothing is more foolish than being the slave of wealth.

That slave thinks he overcomes—when he is overcome.

He thinks he is master—when he is a slave.

Putting bonds on himself, he rejoices.

In making the wild beast fiercer, he is pleased.

He prides himself on becoming a captive, and leaps for joy.

And seeing a rabid dog lunging for his soul, instead of tying up the dog, he actually feeds it plenty of food, that it may leap on him even more fiercely, and become even more of a threat.

As we think on these things, Lord, let us loose the bonds, let us slay the monster, let us drive away the disease, and let us cast out this madness, so we may enjoy a calm and pure health.

Then, when we have sailed into your secure haven, may we all receive your eternal blessings by the grace and love toward man of our Lord Jesus Christ, to whom be glory and might, now and always, and world without end, amen.

—*John Chrysostom*

WE WEEP FOR THOSE WHO LOVE MONEY

Lord, let us mourn with the prophet, and say with him, "Woe to him who builds his palace by unrighteousness, his upper rooms by injustice" (Jeremiah 22:13).

Or rather, let us mourn for those people, as you did, Christ, here on the earth, when you said, "Woe to you who are rich, for you have already received your comfort" (Luke 6:24).

Let us not stop lamenting for the carelessness of our fellow believers. Not for those who have already died (why should we, since we cannot change anything, now), but let us weep for the greedy and the covetous—those who can never get enough.

Lord, we should mourn for those who can still change, even though they might laugh at us while we are lamenting. And that in itself is a good reason to lament—that they would laugh when they ought to be mourning, as well.

For if they had all been affected by our sorrow, we could stop lamenting, since they would promise to change. But since that has not happened, we continue to weep—and not only for the rich, but also for those who are not rich but who desperately want to be. We weep for those who love money, the greedy and grasping.

Lord, we know that wealth in itself is not an evil thing, since we can justifiably spend it on those in need. But greediness is the evil, and it prepares deathless punishments.

So we mourn them. Perhaps they will change. But even if not, others at least might not fall into the same danger, but will guard against it.

Lord, may it come to pass that they will be freed from this sickness, and that none of us will ever fall into it, and that we may all obtain your promised goodness, through the grace and lovingkindness of our Lord Jesus Christ, to whom be glory for ever and ever, amen.

— *John Chrysostom*

HELP ME TO BE CONTENT

For the sake of knowing you, Lord, and for the sake of living in union with you, help me be free of wanting what I should not have.

The economy of your creation is good, and all things are given as they should be given. Nothing happens without a cause.

All-Powerful One, I must be in the center of what is yours. And if I am there, I am near to you. So help me to be free of any fear of drawing near to you. Help me to be satisfied with less. And help me to choose as you would choose between what I want, and what I really need.

Amen.

— *Clement of Alexandria*

FREE US FROM THIS GRIEVOUS BONDAGE

Lord, why do angels not want so many things as we do?

The less we need, the more we are like them. But the more we need, the more we sink down to this perishable life.

We just have to ask those who have grown old which life they deem happiest—when they were helplessly mastered, or now when they are masters of these things?

I mention these persons, Lord, because those who are intoxicated with youth do not even realize their slavery. Will those who have a fever call themselves happy when, thirsting much, they drink much and need more? Or are they happier when they feel better and are free from the desire?

Help us see how needing much is pitiable, and far from true wisdom, and leads to slavery. Why do we bring it upon ourselves?

If it were possible to live uninjured without roof or walls, would we not prefer it? Do we not for this call Adam happy, that he needed nothing—no house, no clothes?

Servants, houses, money ... the more we acquire, the more slavish we become. For absolute freedom is to want nothing at all. The next is to want little. And this the angels and their imitators possess.

We think of how good it would be for us to succeed in this while tarrying in a mortal body. Riches are called "usables," that we may use them rightly, and not keep and bury them. For this is not to possess them, but to be possessed by them.

Help us then to be free from this grievous bondage. Why do we devise ten thousand chains for ourselves? Is not the bond of nature enough, and the necessity of life, and the crowd of affairs? May we not also twine other nets, and put them about our feet!

And when will we lay hold on heaven, and be able to stand on that height? For a great thing is it, that having cut all these cords, we should be able to lay hold of the city which is above. Putting away what does not matter, let us keep to what is necessary.

Thus shall we lay hold of eternal life, through the grace and lovingkindness of our Lord Jesus Christ, to whom be glory forever and ever, amen.

—John Chrysostom

WE FOLLOW YOUR EXAMPLE TO GIVE

Lord, how do we answer when you say, "I was hungry and you gave me nothing to eat" (Matthew 25:42)?

What excuse will we have? We will certainly say we are too poor, yet we are not poorer than the widow who surpassed them all when she gave her two small copper coins.

For you do not require quantity of the offering, but a measure of the mind. And that you do so comes from your tender care.

So as we admire your lovingkindness, let us give what is in our power to give. Since we have received your abundant lovingkindness, both in this life and in the life to come, we may be able to enjoy the good things promised to us, through the grace and lovingkindness of our Lord Jesus Christ. To him be glory for ever and ever, amen.

— *John Chrysostom*

Ours is the kingdom

Lord, you have warned us to watch. And you gave us the
ability to reason, to discover and distinguish good and evil.

You have given us patience not to despair in any hard work
or misfortune. And this should not surprise us, because
you rule well, and you have made us to serve you well.

You have taught us to understand that worldly wealth,
which we once looked upon as our own, is alien and
transitory to us.

You have also taught us to consider as our own what we
once despised and looked upon as foreign: the kingdom
of heaven.

You who have taught us to break no law, and not to mourn
even if we lose our riches, you have taught us to subject
our body to our mind.

Amen.

— *Augustine of Hippo*

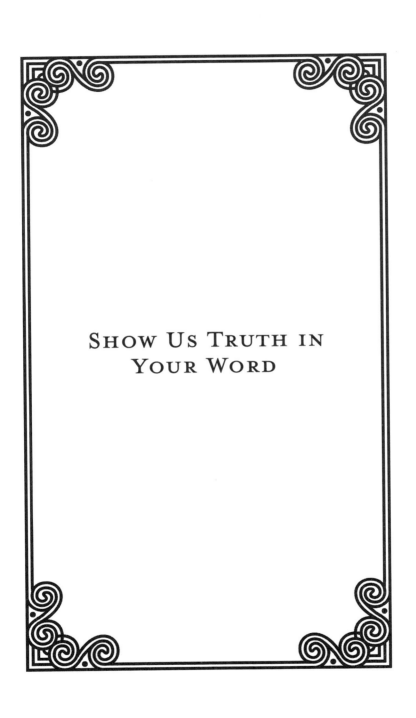

SHOW US TRUTH IN YOUR WORD

WE GREET YOU, O LIGHT!

Sweet is the word that gives us light, precious above gold and gems; it is to be desired above honey and the honeycomb (Psalm 19:10).

How can this word be anything other than desirable, Lord, since it has filled with light the mind which was buried in darkness? This word has sharpened the light-bringing eyes of the soul.

Had it not been for the sun, night would have brooded over the universe—never mind the stars. In the same way, had we not known the word, and been illuminated by him, we would be no different from turkeys that are fed and fattened in darkness, nourished only for death.

Let us then admit the light, that we may admit you, God. Let us admit the light, and become disciples of the Lord. This, too, has been promised to the Father: "I will declare your name to my people; in the assembly will I praise you" (Psalm 22:22).

I once wandered in error, seeking God. But since you led me to the light, O Lord, I have found God through you, and received the Father from you. I have become a co-heir with Christ (Romans 8:17), since you were not ashamed to call me your own.

So help us never to be oblivious to the truth. Help us put away all ignorance. Remove the darkness that obstructs, as dimness of sight, and let us contemplate the only true God as we raise our voices in this hymn of praise:

We greet you, O light! For in us, buried in darkness and hidden within the shadow of death, light has shone forth from heaven, purer than the sun, sweeter than life here below. That light is eternal life, and whoever takes part in that light, lives.

But night fears the light. And hiding itself in terror, it gives way to the day of the Lord.

Sleepless light is now over all, and west defines the east. This is the end result of the new creation, amen.

— *Clement of Alexandria*

ENLIGHTEN MY DARKNESS, LORD

You light my lamp, Lord.

O my God, enlighten my darkness, for by you I will be delivered from temptation. And through my God I will go over a wall.

Amen.

— *John Cassian*

LET ME DIG DEEPER IN THE WORD

Lord, have mercy on me, and hear my desire. It is not
of the earth, and it is not about gold, silver, or precious
stones. It is not about nice clothes, or honors, or a good
position. And it is not about the pleasures of the flesh or
necessaries for the body on this life's pilgrimage.

All these things will be added to those who seek your
kingdom and righteousness. But see, O Lord my God,
here is my desire …

Would you see, Father, and approve? If it pleases you in
your mercy, may I find grace before you, that the inner
parts of your word would be opened to me?

I am knocking.

I ask in the name of Jesus Christ your Son, who is on your
right hand, the Son of Man, who you have established as
your mediator and ours. I ask in the name of him through
whom you sought us, so that we might seek you.

I ask through your Word, through whom you made all
things (and among them, also me). He is the only begotten,
through whom you called believers to adoption (and so
also me).

I ask by him who sits on your right hand, and who
intercedes with you for us, in whom are hidden all the
treasures of wisdom and knowledge.

I seek those treasures in your word. If it pleases you in your mercy, may I find grace before you, that the inner parts of your word would be opened to me?

I am knocking.

— *Augustine of Hippo*

GRANT ME KNOWLEDGE THAT POINTS TO TRUTH

O God Almighty, the Father of your Christ, your only begotten Son, would you give me now an undefiled body, a pure heart, and a watchful mind? Grant me the knowledge that always points to the truth, as well as the influence of the Holy Spirit for gaining and enjoying that truth, in your peace and assurance. I ask this through Jesus Christ, by whom is glory to you, in the Holy Spirit forever, amen.

— *Apostolic Constitutions*

HELP ME KNOW THE TRUTH

Lord, let me hear and understand how in the beginning
you made the heavens and the earth.

Moses wrote this and departed this life. If he were still alive,
I would ask him to explain these things to me, and I would
listen well. And if he spoke to me in Hebrew, I would not
understand. But if in my language, I would understand.

How would I know if what he said was true? Within me,
Truth—in any language, even without voice or tongue,
without the sound of the words—Truth would tell me that
he spoke the truth. I would know it immediately.

But since I cannot ask Moses in person, I ask you, who
are the Truth, and you who filled Moses with truth—you,
my God, I ask you to forgive my sins. You who gave those
truths to Moses to speak, grant to me also that I may
understand them.

Amen.

— Augustine of Hippo

Help us to discover your word

My soul yearns to know this most entangled enigma, Lord.
Please do not shut it away, good Father. I beg you through
Christ, do not close off those familiar and not-so-familiar
things from me.

Do not keep me from entering, but let their light dawn on
me in your mercy.

Who else could I ask? And to whom can I admit my
ignorance? I long to understand your word. I never grow
tired of it.

Please give me what I love, for I do love it. And you have
given me this love, because you know how to give good
gifts to your children. Please grant me understanding,
since I have done my best to understand, and I will
continue in that hard labor until you open the way.

I beg you, through Christ and in his name, let no one
sidetrack me in this. "I believed; therefore I have spoken"
(2 Corinthians 4:13). This is my hope and I live for this:
that I may contemplate the joys of my Lord.

See, you have made my days grow old, and they pass away.
But how it happens, I do not know. We speak of this time
and that time, or ask "How long ago since he did this?" Or,
"How long ago since I saw that?" We say the words and we
understand, but still the real meaning of these things lies
deeply hidden, and we have yet to discover.

Amen.

— *Augustine of Hippo*

Be present in this work

As we lay hands on that head of the deadly serpent, and
as we long to lay hold of all the limbs that are entangled
in the coils of his body, again and again we pray to you,
Lord Jesus.

You are the one we have always prayed to, that you
would give us words by opening our mouth, "to demolish
strongholds [and] arguments and every pretension that
sets itself up against the knowledge of God." We do "take
captive every thought to make it obedient to Christ"
(2 Corinthians 10:4–5).

For that person is indeed free who has begun to be led
captive by you. Be present, then, in this work of yours.
And be present to those of yours who are striving for you,
beyond the measure of their own strength.

Grant to us to bruise the gaping mouth of this new
serpent, and to bruise the neck that swells with deadly
poison. Grant that we may thrust our hands unharmed
into the den of this serpent. And if it has found any holes
to live in the human heart—any place to rest—or if it has
laid any eggs there, or left any trace of its slimy course,
remove it all!

Remove the foul and deadly pollution of lies from that
serpent of lies. Take away the uncleanness that blasphemy
brings, and purify with your sacred cleansing those souls
who are stuck in stinking mud.

I pray that dens of thieves may become houses of prayer, where the gifts of your Holy Spirit and where the beauty of faith and holiness will shine forth.

Pour out the light of compassion and truth upon all those whose eyes have been blinded by stubborn heresy. Help them see with clear and unveiled sight the great and life-giving mystery of your incarnation, how you were born as a human of the virgin, and yet acknowledge that you were always Very God.

Amen.

— *John Cassian*

OPEN OUR HEARTS

Come, Lord, and use your keys. Open, so we understand.

You reveal so much, yet you are not believed. You warn us from the Scriptures, yet are not understood. Where hearts are closed, open and enter in.

"Then he opened their minds so they could understand the Scriptures" (Luke 24:45).

Open, Lord—yes, open the hearts of those who doubt you.

— *Augustine of Hippo*

LET THE WATER PENETRATE MY SOUL

Lord Jesus, this special water that we pour into the basin of our soul, water from the Scriptures, from the Psalms, is the water of the message from heaven.

So let this water penetrate my soul and my flesh, that through the moisture of this rain the valleys of my mind and the field of my heart may grow green.

May your raindrops fall on me, giving grace and eternal life. Wash my mind that I may not sin again and again. Wash the heel of my soul, that I may be able to erase the curse, and not feel the serpent's bite.

You have redeemed the world; redeem the soul of a single sinner.

Amen.

— *Ambrose of Milan*

SET US FREE

HELP US TO FOLLOW AFTER TRUE FREEDOM

Lord, help us to follow after the true freedom—your virtue. Your moral excellence.

Deliver us from that evil slavery. Do not let us count as blessed the dominion of wealth, or pompous power, or any such thing.

What a grievous form of slavery it is, staggering under the weight of passions.

For the only ones who are free, the only ones who are true rulers, the ones who are more kingly than all kings ... are those who are delivered from all their passions.

In you we will enjoy security here in this life and attain the good things to come, by the grace and love toward humanity of our Lord Jesus Christ, to whom be glory and might, with the Father and the Holy Spirit, world without end, amen.

—*John Chrysostom*

You turn evil to nothing

Framer of the universe, grant first that I may call on you.
Please stoop to my level to set me free!

You are God, through whom are all things, which of
themselves were not.

You are the God who keeps from perishing even that
which would destroy itself.

You are the God who created this world out of nothing—a
world which all eyes see is most beautiful.

You do not cause evil, but you limit that evil. And to those
who flee to you for refuge, you turn evil to nothing.

You are the father of truth and wisdom, the father of the
true and crowning life, the father of our awakening, and of
that pledge that bids us return to you.

Amen.

— *Augustine of Hippo*

I HAVE SEEN YOUR SALVATION, LORD

Through him who sits on your throne, and who cannot be separated from your divine nature, you have given us the gift of reconciliation. You have granted us access to you, with confidence.

True and all-powerful God, you recognize no other authority. And you have given these justifying gifts of grace as certain and unquestionable rights to those who have received mercy.

This is what Isaiah meant when he said that "the Angel of his Presence saved them. In his love and compassion he redeemed them; he lifted them up and carried them all the days of old" (Isaiah 63:9).

But all this was not due to any righteous works on our part, or because we loved you. Our forefather Adam turned away from your commands, was judged unworthy of that life-giving place, and from then on the offspring of sin has been so weak.

But you, Lord, by yourself and because of the indescribable love you had toward your creation, you have confirmed your mercy to us. You felt sorry for this separation from you. You were moved by the sight of our degradation, and you took us into compassion.

Now a joyous festival is established for us, Adam's race, because the first creator of Adam has freely become the second Adam. And the brightness of our Lord God has come down to live with us, and we are saved.

I have seen your salvation, Lord. Let me be delivered from the bent yoke of the law. I have seen the eternal King, who has no successors. Let me be free from this burdensome chain of slavery. I have seen him who is by nature my Lord and deliverer, so let me receive his deliverance decree.

Set me free from the yoke of condemnation, and place me under the yoke of justification. Deliver me from the yoke of the curse, from the law that kills, and enroll me in the blessed company of those who, by the grace of your dear Son, who is of equal glory and power with you, have been received into adoption as your children, amen!

— *Methodius of Olympia*

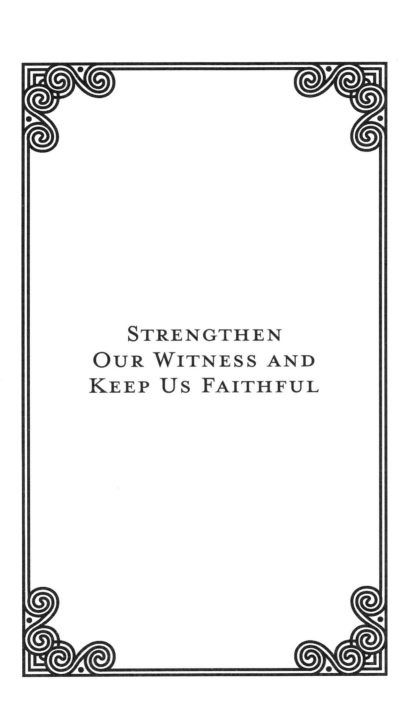

STRENGTHEN OUR WITNESS AND KEEP US FAITHFUL

I owe you my devotion

Lord God Almighty, I know that I owe you the devotion of all my thoughts and words. This is my chief duty in life.

The gift of speech you gave can bring me no higher reward than the opportunity of service in preaching you and showing you as you are—as Father, and Father of God the only-begotten. We proclaim you to the world in its blindness and to the rebellious heretic.

But this is only the expression of my own desire. I pray also for the gift of your help and compassion, that the breath of your Spirit may fill sails I have spread of faith and confession, and that you send your favoring wind to forward me on my voyage of instruction.

We trust the promise of him who said, "Ask, and it will be given to you; seek and you will find; knock and the door will be opened to you" (Matthew 7:7).

In our want, we pray for the things we need. We will bring untiring energy to the study of your prophets and apostles, and we will knock for entrance at every gate of hidden knowledge.

But it is up to you to answer the prayer and grant what we seek. It is up to you to open the door on which we beat. Our minds are born with dull and clouded vision, and our feeble intellect is formed within barriers of ignorance about heavenly things.

Yet the study of what you have revealed in Scripture elevates our soul to understand sacred truth. And submission to the faith is the path to a certainty beyond the reach of reason alone.

So we look to your support as we take the first trembling steps of this undertaking, that it may gain strength and prosper. We look to you to give us the fellowship of that Spirit who guided the prophets and the apostles, that we may take their words in the sense in which they spoke, and assign the right shade of meaning to everything we say.

For we will speak of things which they preached in a mystery—of you, O God Eternal, Father of the Eternal and Only-Begotten God, of you who alone is without birth, and of the one Lord Jesus Christ, born of you from everlasting.

We may not sever him from you, or make him one of many Gods, by saying you are different in nature. We may not say that he is not begotten of you, because you are one. We must not fail to confess him as true God, seeing that he is born of you, his Father.

So grant us precision of language, soundness of argument, grace of style, and loyalty to truth. Enable us to silence the rebellious arguments of heretics, and to say the things we believe, as the prophets and apostles have taught us. And let us confess you, one God our Father, and one Lord Jesus Christ.

Amen.

— *Hilary of Poitiers*

LET ME SPEAK ONLY YOUR WORDS

Lord God, I know it is written that "sin is not ended by multiplying words, but the prudent hold their tongues" (Proverbs 10:19). Help me to speak only by proclaiming your word, and by praising you!

I should please you in whatever I say. For a man you blessed encouraged his true son in the faith to "preach the word" and "be prepared in season and out of season" (2 Timothy 4:2). And the one who spoke "in season and out of season" did not say too much, did he?

Set me free, O God, from too much speech within my soul. I fly for refuge to your mercy, for my thoughts are not silent, even when I say nothing out loud. You know my thoughts. May they not overtake me or lead me to act on them. But at least let my opinions and my conscience be safe from those thoughts, under your protection.

A wise man said, "We speak much, and yet come short; and in sum of words, he is all."

So when we come to you, these many things that we speak, and yet come short, will cease. And you will remain "all in all." In praise we will say one thing without end, when we ourselves are also made one in you.

O Lord the one God, God the Trinity, whatever I have said that is of you, may I acknowledge who are yours, amen.

— *Augustine of Hippo*

GIVE US PATIENCE IN THE HARVEST

Lord, help us to imitate you, and never give up on anyone.

For those who fish, they may have cast many times without success, but when they cast one more time, they gain all.

So we also expect that you will all at once show to us ripe fruit in the lives of others.

The farmer, too, after sowing, waits one or two days, and anticipates a long while ... but all at once the crop springs up on every side.

This we expect will take place also by the grace and lovingkindness of our Lord Jesus Christ, with whom to the Father and also to the Holy Spirit be glory, might, and honor, now and forever and world without end, amen.

— John Chrysostom

CREATE A PEOPLE OF FAITH IN THIS CITY

God the Savior, God of the universe, Lord and creator of the world, Father of the only-begotten Son, you caused him to be the living and true expression of yourself, and sent him for the help of the human race. Through him you called and made us your own possession.

We pray now on behalf of these people.

Send your Holy Spirit on them, and let the Lord Jesus visit them. Let him speak so that all will understand. Soften their hearts to faith, and may Christ himself draw their souls to you, O God of compassion.

Create a people even in this city. Create a genuine flock through your only-begotten, Jesus Christ, in the Holy Spirit—through whom to you is the glory and the strength, now and to all the ages of the ages, amen.

— *Serapion Scholasticus*

You are one God

O God Almighty, I know that you are all-powerful, yet I do not ask that you reveal to me the mystery of that indescribable birth which is secret between yourself and your only-begotten.

Nothing is impossible with you, and I do not doubt that in begetting your Son you exerted your full omnipotence. To doubt it would be to deny that you are omnipotent.

My own birth teaches me that you are good, and therefore I am sure that in the birth of your only-begotten you withheld no good gift. I believe all that is yours is his, and all that is his is yours.

The creation of the world is quite enough evidence to me that you are wise. And I am sure that your Wisdom, who is like you, must have been begotten from you.

You are one God, in very truth, in my eyes. I will never believe that in him, who is God from you, there is anything that is not yours.

Amen.

— Hilary of Poitiers

GIVE US YOUR HAND AND RAISE US UP

Father of the only-begotten, you are good and compassionate. You care for us, lover of humanity and lover of our souls. You are the benefactor of all who turn to you.

Now would you hear this prayer, and give us knowledge and faith, piety, and holiness.

Bring to nothing every passion, every lust, and every sin from among this people. Make us all clean. Have patience with our faults, for we kneel before you, uncreated Father, through the Only-Begotten One.

Give to us your holy understanding and complete support. Enable us to seek and love you, to search and seek out your divine answers.

Master, give us your hand and raise us up.

Raise us up, God of compassions, and cause us to look up. Uncover our eyes and help us to speak.

Do not allow us to be ashamed or embarrassed, or to accuse ourselves. Blot out the charge of the debt that is against us (Colossians 2:14) and write our names in the book of life (Philippians 4:3).

Include us among your holy prophets and apostles, through your only-begotten Jesus Christ, through whom to you is the glory and the strength both now and to all the ages of the ages.

Amen.

— *Serapion Scholasticus*

MAY WE ACT LIKE CHILDREN OF GOD

May we act like children of God, wherever we are, pure and blameless in the midst of a crooked and perverse generation. And may we never be entangled in the snares of the wicked, or bound by the chains of our sins.

May the Word in us never be smothered with the cares of this life, so that we would become unfruitful. But help us to walk on the King's Highway, never turning aside to the right hand or the left, and led by the Spirit through the Straight Gate. Then all that we do will prosper, both now and at the time of judgment, in Christ Jesus our Lord, to whom be glory now and forever, amen.

— *Gregory Nazianzen*

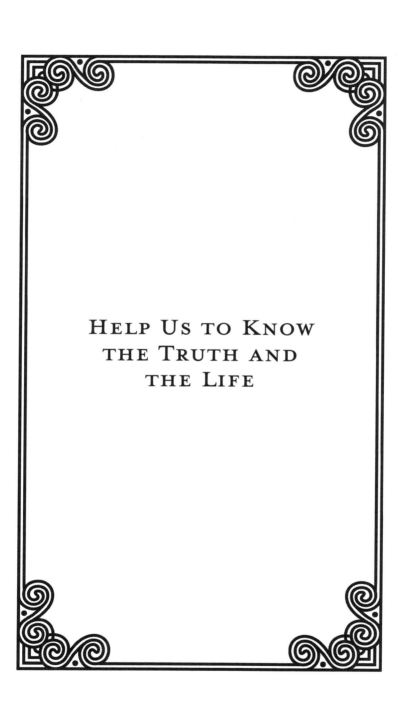

HELP US TO KNOW
THE TRUTH AND
THE LIFE

WE SEE YOU IN CREATION

Lord, grant us the intelligence of your truth, so that we may raise ourselves from visible things to the invisible Being.

May the grandeur and beauty of creatures help us understand you better, the Creator. For the visible things of him from the creation of the world are clearly seen, and your power and divinity are eternal. Earth, air, sky, water, day, night—all visible things remind us of who created and sustains us.

So we will not let sin have a foothold in our lives. We will not allow a place within us for the enemy, if by unbroken recollection we keep God ever dwelling in our hearts.

To you be all glory and all adoration, now and for ever, world without end, amen.

— *Basil of Caesarea*

MAKE US COME ALIVE!

We praise you, unseen Father, provider of immortality.
You are the fountain of life, the fountain of light, and the
fountain of all grace and truth.

Lover of humanity, lover of the poor, you reconcile
yourself to us all. And you draw us all to yourself through
the advent of your beloved Son.

We beg you: Make us come alive! Give us a spirit of light,
that we may "know you, the only true God, and Jesus
Christ, whom you have sent" (John 17:3).

Give us the Holy Spirit, that we may be able to proclaim
your unspeakable mysteries. May the Lord Jesus speak
in us and the Holy Spirit, and may we sing praises to you,
amen.

— *Serapion Scholasticus*

Help us to know the Scriptures

We implore you, Father of the only-begotten, Lord of the universe, the one who has crafted all creatures, the maker of things that have been made.

We stretch out clean hands, and we unfold our thoughts to you, Lord. Have compassion, spare, benefit, improve, and multiply us in virtue, faith, and knowledge.

Visit us, O Lord. We display our own weaknesses to you. Have mercy and pity on us all. Lift up this people, and make us gentle and sober-minded. Cleanse us and set us apart to worship you rightly.

Send your Holy Spirit into our minds and give us grace to learn the Scriptures and to properly interpret their meaning, that others may be encouraged through your only-begotten Jesus Christ in the Holy Spirit, through whom and to you be glory and strength both now and to all the ages of the ages, amen.

— *Serapion Scholasticus*

Enlighten our heart in truth

May the Father of the true light—who has adorned day
with heavenly light, who has made the fire shine which
illuminates us during the night, who reserves for us in
the peace of a future age a spiritual and everlasting light—
enlighten our hearts in the knowledge of truth, keep us
from stumbling, and grant that we may walk honestly as in
the day.

Thus we will shine as the sun in the midst of the glory of
the saints, amen.

— Basil of Caesarea

Make Us One
in the Spirit

KEEP US CLOSE FOREVER

O God, you are faithful and true—you who show your love to a thousand generations of those who love you (Deuteronomy 5:10).

You are the lover of the humble, and the protector of the needy. We all need you. All things are subject to you.

Look down upon this your people, those who bow down their heads to you, and bless them with spiritual blessing.

Keep us as the apple of your eye (Psalm 17:8). Preserve us in complete devotion to you, and in right living before you.

And grant us eternal life in Christ Jesus your beloved Son, with whom glory, honor, and worship be to you and to the Holy Spirit, now and always, forever and ever. Amen.

— *Apostolic Constitutions*

Keep my devotion pure

Lord, I pray that you will keep pure my devotion to you.

Even until my spirit departs, let me describe my convictions this way, so that I will always hold fast the truths I confessed in the creed of my regeneration, when I was baptized in the name of the Father, Son, and Holy Spirit.

Let me adore you, Father, and your Son together with you. And let me win the favor of your Holy Spirit, who is from you through the Only-Begotten One.

For I have a convincing witness to my faith, who said, "All I have is yours, and all you have is mine. And glory has come to me through them" (John 17:10).

It is my Lord Jesus Christ, who abides in you, and is from you, and is with you.

He is forever God who is blessed forever and ever, amen.

— *Hilary of Poitiers*

Send your Spirit

God of all, who spoke by the Holy Spirit through the prophets, you sent forth the Spirit upon the apostles on the day of Pentecost.

Now send forth the Spirit upon us at this time, and by the Spirit also keep us. Impart his benefits in common to us all, that we may always show forth the fruits of the Spirit: love, joy, peace, forbearance, kindness, goodness, faithfulness, gentleness, and self-control (Galatians 5:22–23).

In Christ Jesus our Lord, by whom and with whom, together with the Holy Spirit, be glory to the Father, both now and ever, and forever and ever, amen.

— *Cyril of Jerusalem*

Gather your church, Lord

Almighty and everlasting God, just as grain was once scattered, but has now been gathered and baked into one loaf, so would you also gather your church from the ends of the earth and bring them into your kingdom?

Our Father, we also thank you for the precious blood of Jesus Christ, which was shed for us, and for his precious body, which we celebrate and portray here—just as he himself commanded, to "proclaim the Lord's death until he comes" (1 Corinthians 11:26).

For through him glory is to be given you forever, amen.

— *Apostolic Constitutions*

PROTECT US FROM SIN AND EVIL

FIGHT FOR ME AGAINST SATAN AND HIS HOST

Lord Jehovah, judge my cause and fight for me against Satan and his host. Lay the strong one low!

I have cast off his yoke, and renounced his cursed power. He doubly hates this, and longs to seize me as his prey.

I flee to you and to your cross for help. He would win if you did not deliver me—but you have already defeated him.

Do not let him conquer me! Put him to shame, O Lord my God! Give me the victory!

It is not strength that wins; my weakness is my shield. In lowly trust we fight the fight, and weakness wins the battle.

So give me a lowly heart, and cast away each prideful thought. Let gentleness and love come in instead, and abide in my life.

Your will, not mine, be done. I resist my selfish desires. Let me ever and always be your servant only.

Jesus, I flee to you. I cling to your cross. Save me from Satan's hellish power and pluck me from his grasp.

So I will praise you, Lord, and adore your great name. With Father and Spirit one, forever and ever, amen.

— *Ephraim the Syrian*

FOR VICTORY OVER THE EVIL ONE

You have bound the strong man, and spoiled all that was in his house, you who have given us power over all the power of the enemy. You have delivered the serpent, that murderer, bound to us, as a sparrow to children.

You have cast him down like lightning from heaven to earth, from honor to dishonor.

For all things fear you, and tremble before the face of your power. You look upon the earth, and it trembles. You touch the mountains, and they smoke. You threaten the sea, and it dries up, and you make all rivers like the desert.

The clouds are the dust of your feet, and you walk upon the sea as if it were firm ground.

You are the only begotten God, the Son of the great Father.

Rebuke these wicked spirits, and deliver the works of your hands from the power of the adverse spirit.

For your truth remains forever. Infants praise you, and angels sing hymns to you. To you is due glory, honor, and worship, by you to your Father, in the Holy Spirit, forever, amen.

— *Apostolic Constitutions*

Let us not sink into sin

Lord, the way of life is narrow, and the way of anguish is broad. But prayer can bring us to the house of the kingdom.

We know that pure prayer is perfect work. In comparison, our best efforts are nothing; our hard work is empty conceit.

Only through your grace can we become good in our nature. Only through your righteousness can we become righteous. Only through your mercy and favor can we go from dust to someone in your image.

Grant us the strength to not sink into sin. And make us aware: Pour memory into our hearts that we may always know your honor. Pour truth into our minds, so we do not perish in doubt. Occupy our understanding with your law, so we do not wander in useless thoughts. Order our steps, so we do not hurt ourselves.

Let us draw near to you, that Satan would flee.

When passions are cast from our hearts, see? The enemy flies away. Help us to hate sin and wickedness, and Satan will flee at once.

Because whatever sins we serve become secret idols. With whatever transgressions we love, we worship demons in our soul. If we come against fellow believers, Satan lives there in peace. Envy of others gives rest to devils. And if we tell of the shortcomings of others who are not present, our tongues have become a harp for the devil's music.

Any time we harbor hatred in our souls, we add to the great peace of the deceiver. And if we love the occult, we come against you. Improper talk prepares a feast for demons.

This is the worship of idols, the lusts of the flesh. Grant us the strength to not sink into sin.

Amen.

— Ephraim the Syrian

EQUIP US TO FIGHT THE ENEMY

Do not let us avoid the reading of the divine Scriptures, Lord. For that would be of Satan's devising—not wanting us to see the treasure, otherwise we would gain the riches. So he would say that hearing the divine laws means nothing. Otherwise, if we did, we might become doers of the word, as well as hearers.

Knowing then his evil plan, Lord, let us fortify ourselves against him on every side. Fenced with this kind of armor, we can live unconquered lives, as well as strike a heavy blow to his head.

Then, crowned with glorious wreaths of victory, we can attain the good things to come, by the grace and love toward others of our Lord Jesus Christ, to whom be glory and might for ever and ever, amen.

— John Chrysostom

Keep me far from the snares

In a vast wilderness full of snares and dangers, look! At your enabling I have cut off many of them, thrusting them out of my heart. And yet so many of these things buzz on all sides about my daily life.

Do I dare say that nothing of this sort catches my attention, or causes even the slightest interest?

True, I do not spend time in the worst kinds of entertainment, I do not dabble in astrology or the occult. I detest all those sacrilegious mysteries. And I owe you my humble and singlehearted service, O Lord my God.

Yet the enemy, with tricks and suggestions, looks for a way in.

So I beg you, by our King, even if I am far away from consenting to the enemy, may it ever be farther and farther away.

You enable me, and will enable me, to follow you willingly, doing what you want me to do.

Amen.

— Augustine of Hippo

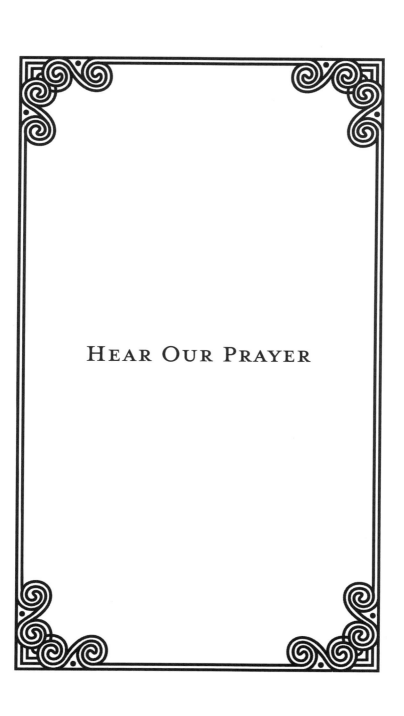

HEAR OUR PRAYER

ACCEPT OUR SACRIFICES OF PRAYER

Lord, you have fulfilled the promises made by the
prophets. You have had mercy on Zion, and compassion
on Jerusalem. You have lifted high the throne of
your servant David, through the birth of Christ—his
descendant according to the flesh.

So now accept the prayers of your people, even the
gentiles who call on you in truth—just as you accepted the
gifts of the righteous, in their generations.

You respected the sacrifice of Abel, the sacrifice of Noah
when he left the ark, of Abraham when he went out of the
land of the Chaldeans, of Isaac at the Well of the Oath, of
Jacob in Bethel, of Moses in the desert, of Aaron between
the dead and the living, of Joshua in Gilgal, of Gideon at
the rock, of Manoah and his wife in the field, of Samson
in his thirst, of Jephtha before his rash vow, of Barak and
Deborah in the days of Sisera.

You respected the sacrifice of Samuel in Mizpeh, of
David at the threshing floor, of Solomon in Gibeon and
Jerusalem, of Elijah in Mount Carmel, of Elisha at the
barren fountain, of Jehoshaphat in war, of Hezekiah in
sickness, of Manasseh in the land of the Chaldeans, of
Josiah, of Ezra at the return, of Daniel in the den of lions,
of Jonah in the whale's belly, of the three in the fiery
furnace, of Hannah in the tabernacle, of Nehemiah at the
rebuilding of the walls, of Zerubbabel, of Mattathias and
his sons, and of Jael in blessings.

Now also receive the prayers of your people, offered to
you with knowledge, through Christ in the Spirit.

Amen.

— Apostolic Constitutions

FULFILL THE DESIRES OF YOUR SERVANTS

Almighty God, you have given us grace at this time to be
able to pray all together to you for our common needs.
You have promised that when two or three are gathered
in your name, you will grant their requests. Fulfill now,
O Lord, the desires and requests of your servants, in a way
that is best for them. Grant us in this world knowledge of
your truth, and in the world to come life everlasting.

Amen.

— John Chrysostom

24 HOURS OF PRAYER

1 a.m. O Lord, do not deprive us of your heavenly blessings.

2 a.m. O Lord, deliver me from eternal torment.

3 a.m. O Lord, if I have sinned in my mind or thought, in word or in deed, forgive me.

4 a.m. O Lord, help me never to be ignorant or careless. Deliver me from pettiness of the soul or stony hardness of heart.

5 a.m. O Lord, deliver me from every temptation.

6 a.m. O Lord, enlighten my heart, where it is darkened by evil desires.

7 a.m. O Lord, I, being a human being, have sinned. You, being God, do please forgive me in your lovingkindness, for you know the weakness of my soul.

8 a.m. O Lord, send down your grace to help me, that I may glorify your holy name.

9 a.m. O Lord Jesus Christ, inscribe me, your servant, in the book of life, and grant me a blessed end.

10 a.m. O Lord my God, even if I have done nothing good in your sight, yet grant me, according to your grace, that I may make a start in doing good.

11 a.m. O Lord, sprinkle on my heart the dew of your grace.

12 noon. O Lord of heaven and earth, remember me, your sinful servant, cold of heart and impure, in your kingdom.

1 p.m. O Lord, I repent; please receive me.

2 p.m. O Lord, do not leave me.

3 p.m. O Lord, save me from temptation.

4 p.m. O Lord, grant me pure thoughts.

5 p.m. O Lord, grant me tears of repentance, remembrance of death, and the sense of peace.

6 p.m. O Lord, grant me mindfulness to confess my sins.

7 p.m. O Lord, grant me humility, compassion toward others, and obedience.

8 p.m. O Lord, help me to be tolerant, magnanimous, and gentle.

9 p.m. O Lord, implant in me the root of all blessings: the fear of you in my heart.

10 p.m. O Lord, grant that I may love you with all my heart and soul, and that I may obey your will in all things.

11 p.m. O Lord, shield me from evil persons and devils and passions and all other lawless matters.

12 midnight. O Lord, you know your creation and what you have willed for it. May your will also be fulfilled in me, a sinner, for you are blessed forevermore. Amen.

—*John Chrysostom*

THOUGH OUR BODIES DECAY, WE SERVE YOU

All the creatures you created serve you, Lord. At your command the heavens turn and the stars hold their courses. The sun brings the bright day, and the moon brings light by night.

You establish the year by the changes of the four seasons. And so all the stars change and vary in the same way, the sea and the rivers ... all creation changes. Yet some come again differently, as leaves on trees. Like apples and grass, plants grow old and dry, and others grow and ripen in their place.

Even our bodies grow old, just as other creatures. But just as we are worth more than trees or other animals, so we will arise more worthily on the day of judgment, so that never afterward will our bodies come to nothing or get old. And though this body had decayed, yet our soul was ever-living since first it was created.

Lord, you prepare the wellspring of every good, and you shield us against every evil. Nothing is above you. You created us in your own image.

Hear me, O Lord, for you are my God and my Lord, my Father, and my creator. You are my governor and my hope, my riches and my honor, my house and my inheritance. You are my salvation and my life. Hear me, O Lord.

I am your servant.

Amen.

— *Augustine of Hippo*

To the creator of everything

O Lord, creator of all things, show me first how to pray to you properly and acceptably.

I call on you, Lord—maker of everything that could not have sprung into being on its own. None of us can even live without you.

I call on you, Lord—who leaves none of your creatures to become nothing.

I call on you who have made all creatures beautiful, from nothing.

I call on you who has never created anything evil, but rather every good work.

I call on him who teaches a few wise ones that evil is nothing.

Amen.

— *Augustine of Hippo*

GIVE US KINGDOM THOUGHTS

We turn to you, Lord God, Father Almighty. And with pure hearts we offer to you our best and truest thanks, as much as we can in our weakness.

With all of our hearts we pray for your exceeding kindness. In your good pleasure, stoop down to hear our prayers, and drive out the enemy from our thoughts and actions.

Increase our faith, guide our understanding, give us kingdom thoughts, and lead us to your spiritual joy— through Jesus Christ your Son, our Lord, who lives and reigns with you in the unity of the Holy Spirit, one God forever and ever, amen.

— Augustine of Hippo

KEEP US FOCUSED ON ETERNITY

PREPARE US FOR ETERNITY

You who overcame death when you yourself arose, and who also will make every person arise...

You who makes us worthy of you, and cleanses us from all our sins, and makes us right in your presence, and hears our prayers...

You who brought us into your household, and always teaches us your good ways, and does us good, and does not abandon us to serve an evil lord, as we once did...

You call us back to the right way, and you lead us to the door, and open it to us, and give us the bread of eternal life and the drink of life's well.

You who warns us away from sin, and teaches us to judge rightly, and then to do righteousness...

You strengthened us, and still do, in our belief, so unbelievers will not harm us.

You have given us, and still do give us, understanding to overcome the error of those who teach that there is no reward or accountability after death.

You who have released us from slavery, you have prepared eternal life for us, and prepared us for eternal life. Amen.

— *Augustine of Hippo*

BRING US TO YOUR PLACE OF BLESSINGS

Lord God, as we turn to you in purity of heart, we give
you our highest and most abundant thanks, as best we are
able in our frailty.

Our whole mind prays for your unmatched goodness, that
by your power you would drive out the enemy from our
thoughts and deeds.

Father Almighty, enlarge our faith, direct our minds, and
help us to focus our thoughts on your kingdom.

And in the end, bring us safe to your place of endless
blessings, through your Son Jesus Christ, amen.

— Augustine of Hippo

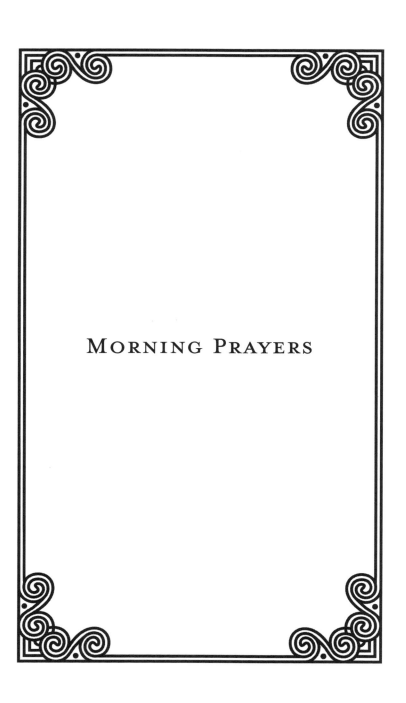

MORNING PRAYERS

You alone are our King

"Glory to God in the highest heaven, and on earth peace to those on whom his favor rests" (Luke 2:14).

We praise you, we sing to you, we bless you, we glorify you, we worship you by your great high priest, Jesus Christ—you who are the true God, who are the One Unbegotten, the only Inaccessible One.

For your great glory, O Lord and heavenly King, O God the Father Almighty, O Lord God, the Father of Christ the Lamb without sin, who takes away the sin of the world, receive our prayer.

For you alone are holy. You only are the Lord Jesus, the Christ of the God of all created nature.

You alone are our King. We give you all glory, honor, and worship!

— *Apostolic Constitutions*

RECEIVE OUR MORNING THANKSGIVING

O God of spirits and of all flesh, God who is beyond compare, and who stands in need of nothing, you have given the sun to rule over the day, and the moon and the stars to rule over the night.

Now would you also look down upon us with gracious eyes, and receive our morning thanksgiving? Have mercy upon us; we have not "spread out our hands to a foreign god" (Psalm 44:20).

For there is no new god among us. You, the eternal God, are without end. You have given us our being through Christ, and our well-being through him.

Grant us also, through him, eternal life. We give glory, honor, and worship to you and to the Holy Spirit forever.

Amen.

— Apostolic Constitutions

I AM NO LONGER SILENT

To you, O Christ, I offer my praise as the firstfruits of my daily work.

For you arose from the dead on this joyous day, flinging open the gates of hell and breaking the power of death, robbing death of its sting. You rushed from the tomb, appearing to those for whom you died and rose again, so that we, newborn, might also rise, set free from death.

Now we will live forever with you, our ascending Lord.

Heaven is ringing today with glad praises, while a choir of angels sings crowning anthems.

Though silent before, today I let loose in song to you. My breath and my instruments belong to you!

Words to the true Word, mind to Mind, today I offer what I could afford. But from here on, if you will, I want to bring a more worthy offering.

Amen.

— *Gregory Nazianzen*

FILL OUR HEARTS WITH JOY AND GLADNESS

You are blessed, O Lord. You are the one who has fed and nourished me since I was young, and who gives food to all living things.

Fill our hearts now with joy and gladness. And, since we always have enough, may we then abound to do every good work, in Christ Jesus our Lord, through whom glory, honor, and power be to you forever, amen.

— Apostolic Constitutions

YOU RAISED ME TO FACE THE MORNING

As I rise from sleep I thank you, Holy Trinity. Through your great goodness and patience you were not angry with me, a sinner who fails to act.

You have not destroyed me in my sins, but have shown your love for humanity once again. When I was flat on my face in despair, you raised me to face the morning and to glorify your power.

Now enlighten my mind's eye and open my mouth to study your word and understand your commands. Help me to do your will and sing to you in heartfelt adoration and praise, to your most holy name—Father, Son, and Holy Spirit, now and forever unto the ages of ages, amen.

— Basil of Caesarea

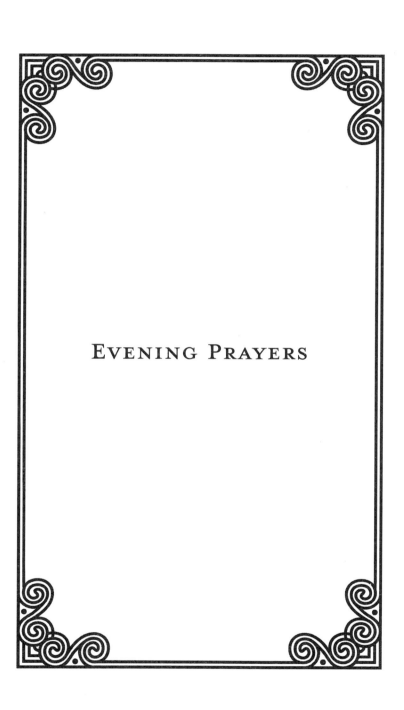

EVENING PRAYERS

HAIL GLADDENING LIGHT!

Hail, gladdening Light, of his pure glory poured
Who is the immortal Father, heavenly, blest,
Holiest of Holies, Jesus Christ our Lord!

Now we are come to the sun's hour of rest;
The lights of evening round us shine;
We hymn the Father, Son, and Holy Spirit divine!

Worthiest are you at all times to be sung
With undefiled tongue,
Son of our God, giver of life, alone:
Therefore in all the world your glories, Lord, they own.

— *Athenogenes*

WE BLESS YOU THIS EVENING

Praise the name of the Lord.

We praise you. We sing songs of worship to you. We
bless you for your great glory, O Lord our King, the
Father of Christ the sinless Lamb, who takes away the sin
of the world.

Praise becomes you. Hymns become you. Glory becomes
you, our God and Father, through the Son, in the most
Holy Spirit, forever and ever, amen.

— *Apostolic Constitutions*

THANKS FOR THE EVENING

O God, you are without beginning and without end. You are the maker of the whole world by Jesus Christ. You are the provider, but before all, you are his God and Father, the Lord of the Spirit. You are the King of all those who think and speak.

You have made the day for the works of light, and the night for the refreshment of our weakness.

Lord, lover of humanity, and fountain of all that is good, would you now in your mercy accept the thanksgiving we offer?

You have brought us through the length of the day, and to the beginnings of the night. Preserve us by your Christ, allow us an evening of peace, and a night free from sin.

And grant us everlasting life by your Christ, through whom glory, honor, and worship be to you in the Holy Spirit forever. Amen.

— *Apostolic Constitutions*

PROTECT US TONIGHT

Creator of earth and sky, you rule the heavens. You clothe the day with robes of light, and bless us at night with gracious sleep.

Your rest gives us comfort in our weariness, and refreshes us to work again in the morning. You soothe our harried minds, and you take away our heavy loads of sorrow.

The day passes. We thank you for your gift. We lift our prayers, vows, and songs to you each night. We need your shield and protection.

Shadows may close around us, but faith knows no darkness. The night borrows from the brightness of its clear spotlight.

We pray to you, Father, Son, and Spirit—three in one, blessed Trinity. Guard your sheep by day and night.

Amen.

— *Ambrose of Milan*

THIS EVENING I COME TO BLESS YOU

Christ, my Lord, I come now to bless you, when the day is veiled in night. You who know no beginning. You, light of the eternal light.

You dissolve the darkness, creating the light, so that everything may be in the light.

You fixed the unfixed chaos, molding it into wondrous beauty for us to see.

You gave humanity a way to reason, far beyond other speechless creatures. See? We are a light in your light, and we should become wholly light.

You have placed bright lamps in the radiant heavens, filling the skies above. Day and night serve you in love.

Now, at night our weary natures find rest from tears and toil. But in the morning, Lord, we will return to the work that pleases you.

So wake us when the day appears.

Amen.

— *Gregory Nazianzen*

I LIFT MY EYES TO YOU IN THE EVENING

The day is over and past.

All thanks be to you, O Lord. I pray that the dark hours may not bring their trouble. Jesus, keep me in your sight, and save me through the coming night.

The joys of the day are over.

I lift my heart to you, O Jesus. Would you make the darkness as light, and keep me safe through the coming night?

The work of the day is over.

I sing to you now in praise, and ask that you make safe the hours of fear. Jesus, keep me in your sight, and guard me through the coming night.

Lighten mine eyes, O Savior, or I would sleep in death. And the one who tempts me by day would cry in triumph, "He could not make the darkness light, or guard them through the night!"

So be the preserver of my soul, O God—you know the dangers I must go through.

Hear my prayer, lover of humanity! Guard and save me from all, amen.

— *Anatolius of Constantinople*

BRING BACK THE LIGHT

Divine Word of truth, today I have not been all light. I
have not kept the day as completely and wholly yours. You
have seen the dark spots of failure.

Now the sun has set and the night has won. I have worked
against you, my Lord. I vowed and thought to do, but
failed. My steps slid somewhere else.

Darkness came from below, obscuring the way of safety.

Bring back your light, O Christ.

Turn darkness into day.

Amen.

— *Gregory Nazianzen*

PRAYERS FOR CHURCH LIFE

Hear these new believers, Lord

Lord, in your mercy, hear the prayers of these believers. Give them the desires of their hearts, for their good. Reveal to them the gospel, give them understanding, lead them in the knowledge of God, and implant in them awe and reverence for you.

Open the ears of their hearts, that they may grow in your ways, day and night.

Strengthen them in right living, and unite them with others in your church. Help them to grow into a life of faith. Clothe them in your garment of virtue and purity, which is true life. Deliver them from ungodliness, and allow no place to the adversary who is against them.

Cleanse them from all filthiness of flesh and spirit. Dwell in them and walk in them, through Jesus Christ.

Bless them as they come and go, and order their everyday affairs for their good. Grant them your peace through Jesus Christ, free from sin.

Almighty and only true God and Father of Jesus Christ, God of the Comforter, Lord of the whole world, look down now on these your servants as they learn and grow in the gospel. Give them a new heart, and renew a right spirit within them, that they may know and do your will with all their hearts and a willing soul.

Join and unite them to this body, your church, and show them your mysteries through Christ, our hope, who died for them and by whom glory and worship be given you in the Holy Spirit forever, amen.

— *Apostolic Constitutions*

For those who are baptized

Lord God, you have always been and always will be. You are uncreated and there is no one greater.

Lord of the whole world, who has spread the sweet aroma of the knowledge of the gospel among the nations, spread that gospel now upon those who are being baptized. May the sweet aroma of Jesus Christ remain on us. Now that we have died with him, may we arise and live with him, as well.

Let those who have been dead with Christ, and who are now raised up with him, stand up and pray! And let us praise and thank you as they did after the temple of the Lord was finished by King Solomon, saying, "He is good; his love endures forever" (2 Chronicles 7:3).

— *Apostolic Constitutions*

ON THE DEATH OF A CHILD

Lord, how bitter is the grief for a child who dies, and for the separation of the youngest ones from their mothers.

Train up these little ones, Lord, in your dwelling place.

This day afflicts fathers through their sons, and death now breaks the cane of old age.

Lord, may they now lean on you.

This day removes the beloved ones from their mothers, and takes away the arms which would have been her support.

May she trust in you, Lord.

This day separates the little ones from their parents, and leaves those parents behind in the wilderness of suffering and grief.

Comfort them, Lord.

This day divides nursing children from their mothers, who are left now to cry and grieve at the connection that was lost.

May mother and child reunite in your kingdom.

Happy the infancy that gains paradise—but oh, we who grow old without them, we remain in sorrow.

Lord, be our helper. Amen.

— *Ephraim the Syrian*

ON THE DEATH OF A FRIEND

Lord and Maker of all things—including our human bodies...

God and Father, pilot of those who are yours...

Lord of life and death...

Judge and benefactor of our souls...

Maker and transformer of all things by your designing Word, in your due time, according to the depth of your wisdom and providence...

Receive now our friend, the firstfruits of our pilgrimage.

If he who was last is first, we bow before your Word, by which the universe is ruled.

Receive us also afterward, in your time, for as long as you need us here on earth.

Receive us, prepared and untroubled, faithful to the end, not clinging to things here, like souls fond of the world and the flesh.

Instead, we would be filled with eagerness for that blessed and enduring life which is in Christ Jesus, our Lord, to whom be glory, world without end, amen.

— *Gregory Nazianzen*

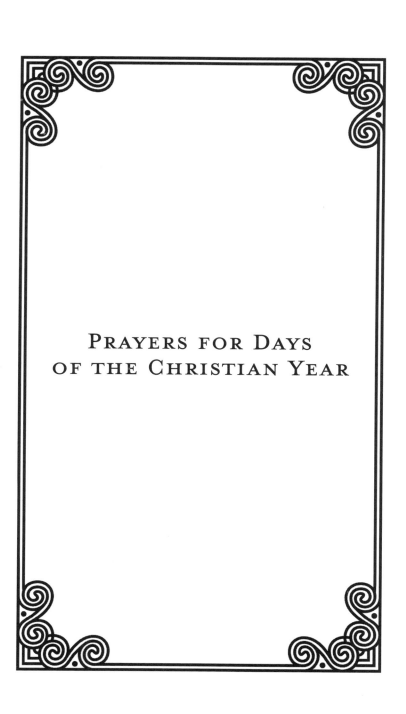

PRAYERS FOR DAYS
OF THE CHRISTIAN YEAR

LORD, GIVE US PEACE

(A Sabbath prayer)

O Lord, give us peace, for you have given us all things.

The peace of rest. The peace of the Sabbath, which has no evening.

For all the wonderful array of creation was very good, but it will pass away when its course is finished. For in it was morning and evening.

But the seventh day has no evening, and no setting. You have set it apart to continue forever. After all your very good works, you rested. You made them in unbroken rest.

So may the voice of your book announce to us that, after all our works (very good works, because you gave them to us), we will rest in you in the sabbath of eternal life.

Then you will rest in us, as you are now working in us. That will be your rest through us, even as these are your works through us.

But you, Lord, work forever, even as you rest forever. You do not see things through the lens of time. You do not rest in time. And yet you make things to be seen in time, and time itself, and the rest that results from time.

So we see those things you made, because they are. But they are, because you see them. And we see how they are good, inside and out. You see them as they are made, but also you saw them, yet to be made.

With our hearts now filled with the Spirit, we do well. In the past, we were moved to do evil, forsaking you. But you, the One, the good God, never stopped doing good.

And we also own good gifts from you, though they are not eternal, and after them we trust we will rest in your great holiness.

But you, being the good who needs no good, are now forever at rest, because your rest is you yourself. Who can teach another to understand this? Or what angel can teach other angels, or people?

So we will continue to ask of you, seek in you, and knock. So it will be received, so it will be found, and so it will be opened, amen.

— *Augustine of Hippo*

THIS DAY YOU MADE TO REST

(A Sabbath prayer)

Lord Almighty, you have created the world by Christ, and have appointed the Sabbath as a way for us to remember. This is the day you made for us to rest from our work and meditate on your laws.

You have also established festivals for the rejoicing of our souls, so we can remember the wisdom you created: how you came to earth for us, how you appeared in life and were baptized, how you came as God and man both, how you allowed Jesus to suffer for us, die, and rise again in your power.

For this reason we solemnly gather on the Lord's day to celebrate the feast of the resurrection. We rejoice because of him who conquered death and brought us life and immortality.

For by Jesus Christ you have brought those who were not Jews into the family of God, now a dedicated people for yourself—the true Israel, beloved of God, who see God.

For you brought our fathers out of the land of Egypt. You delivered them out of the furnace, and from clay- and brick-making. You redeemed them out of the hands of Pharaoh, and of those under him, and led them through the sea as through dry land. You brought them through the wilderness and blessed them with good things.

You gave them the Ten Commandments, pronounced by your voice and written with your hand. You commanded them to observe the Sabbath, not as a day for idleness, but as an opportunity for devotion, a chance to experience your power, and a way to keep away evil. You gave them holy protection for the sake of holy truth.

So you allowed us all to rest on the Sabbath, that we might speak no angry words. For the Sabbath is when creation ceases, and the world is complete. On the Sabbath we focus on God's law and give him grateful praise for his blessings.

The Lord's day commands us to thank you for everything, O Lord. For this is your great grace that even overshadows all other blessings.

Amen.

— *Apostolic Constitutions*

GLORY TO YOUR COMING, WHICH MADE US ALIVE *(A Christmas prayer)*

Blessed be the child who made Bethlehem glad on this day! And glory to your coming, which made us alive again.

Glory to the hidden gardener of our minds. His seed fell on our ground and made our minds rich.

Glory to the silence, who spoke by his voice. To the hidden one, whose son was made known. To the great one, whose son descended and was small. To the living one, whose son was made to die.

Glory to the son of the good one, whom the sons of the evil one rejected. To the son of the just one, whom the sons of wickedness crucified. And glory to the one who set us free, and was bound for us all.

Glory to him who gave the pledge, and redeemed it, too. To the beautiful one, who conformed us to his image. To him on high, who mixed his salt in our minds, and his leaven in our souls. Whose body became bread to bring our deadness alive.

Praise to the rich one, who paid for us all.

Glory to him who can never be measured. Our heart is too small, our mind too feeble. You make foolish our littleness by the riches of your wisdom.

Thanks be to him who sent his heir, that by him he might draw us to himself, and even make us heirs with him. Thanks be to the good one, the cause of all goods.

Blessed is the shepherd who became a lamb for our salvation. The branch who became the cup of our redemption. The architect who became our tower of safety.

Let us praise him whose wounds made us alive, and who took away the curse by his thorns. Praise him who put death to death by his dying, who went to sleep and chased our deep sleep away.

Glory to him who was baptized, and drowned our iniquity in the deep. Who choked the one that was choking us.

Blessed be the one who made in the womb a perfect temple, that he might dwell in it, a throne that he might be in it, a garment that he might be arrayed in it, and a weapon that he might conquer in it.

Blessed be him whom our mouth cannot adequately praise. His gift is too great for the skill of orators to tell. Praise him as we may, it is too little. And since it is useless to be silent and constrain ourselves, may our feebleness excuse whatever praise we can sing.

How gracious you are—you expect not more than our strength can give. Ocean of glory who needs not to have your glory sung, accept in your goodness this drop, amen.

— Ephraim the Syrian

WHAT DO WE CALL YOU, LORD?

(A Christmas prayer)

I am not sure what to call you, Child of the Living One.
Not the child of Joseph; you are not actually his blood.
And while you are the son of one, I should be calling you
the son of many.

Ten thousand names would not be enough to call you,
since you are the Son of God and also the Son of Man.
You are David's son and Mary's Lord.

For your sake Mary also was hated. The one who
conceived you was persecuted. The sea raged against her,
as it did against Jonah. Herod, that raging wave, sought to
drown the Lord of the seas.

But Adam would rejoice, for you are the key to paradise.
So I will flee with you, that I may gain life wherever we
go. Prison with you is no prison, because we gain heaven
through you.

With you, the grave is no grave, for you are the resurrection!

Amen.

— *Ephraim the Syrian*

WHO ARE YOU, THAT YOU LOVE US
SO MUCH? *(A Christmas prayer)*

How meek you are, Jesus, yet how mighty! Your judgment is mighty, but your love is sweet. Who can stand against you?

If we seek who you really are, your true nature is hidden in heaven, in the essence of the mighty Triune God. But if a person were to seek your face, they could have found you in the lap of Mary.

Who can realize your depth, you who are a great sea that made itself so small? We come to see you as God, and see? You were a man! Or if we came to see you as a man, the light of your Godhead shone brightly.

Who would believe that you are the heir of David's throne? From all his beds, you inherited an animal's feeding trough. From his palaces you received a cave. And instead of his chariots, a young donkey.

How fearless you are, allowing everyone to carry you in their arms. You met all with a smile, making no distinction between family and stranger, between your mother and others.

Was it your love—you, who love all? What moved you to let everyone have you, the rich and the poor alike? How could you not return anger for anger, fear for threat? You are above returning injury for injury.

Who are you, Jesus, that you love us so much?

Amen.

— *Ephraim the Syrian*

Glory to you who became lowly

(A Christmas prayer)

What mere human can declare the glory of the All-Life-Giver, who stepped down from majesty and humbled himself to become humanity?

You who lifted up humanity in your birth, lift up my weak mind to declare your birth and proclaim your grace.

How amazing is it that the Son dwelled completely in a body, that it was enough for him. Your will was fully contained, yet your bounds reached wholly to the Father. Blessed be he who, though without bounds, was bound!

Who can explain how, though you dwelled wholly in a body, you also dwelled wholly in all?

Your majesty is concealed from us, while your grace is revealed before us. I will be silent, O Lord of majesty, and I will tell of your grace. Your grace clung to you, while it bowed you down to our worst.

Your grace made you a baby, and your grace made you a man. Your grace straightened and enlarged your majesty. Blessed is the might that became little ... and became great!

Glory to you who became lowly, though your nature is lofty. By your own will you became man, though you are God by nature. Blessed be your glory which put on our image!

Your hope brought new hope when ours had broken down.
Blessed be the one who brought good news of hope!

Double was the happiness of those who saw your birth
and your day, yet also happy are those who have not seen,
but who have believed. Blessed is your happiness that is
added to us!

Amen.

— *Ephraim the Syrian*

MAY THE FIRST DAY OF YOURS BE

BLESSED *(A Christmas prayer)*

May the first day of yours be blessed, Lord—the day from which this feast day is stamped. This day is like you: it shows us mercy, and it is handed down from generation to generation. This day refreshes itself by its love. After it visits, and passes, and goes away, in mercy it returns and visits us again.

We need this day; our human nature needs it. The world needs the fountain of this day. We are thirsty for this day, just as we are thirsty for you.

This is the day that rules the seasons! On your day, Lord—a day that is near to us—we see your birth that is far off.

For your day reconciled heaven and earth. The highest came down to the lowest. Your mercy shone forth on the guilty. Great is your day, Lord! Let mercy shine forth on us sinners. And if your forgiveness wells up every other day, how much more today.

Let us distinguish your day from all days, for great is the treasure house of the day of your birth. On this day mercy came forth to sinners. On this day the medicine of life came to the wounded, and the light shone on our blindness.

Voice of the Father, the world is noisy. Our mind wanders. Make still those other voices, and let us find quiet in you. For by you the sea was stilled from its storms.

And let your flock rejoice. Let your day, O Lord, give us all joy, joy with the flowers of peace. Keep the glory of your birth, today.

Amen.

— Ephraim the Syrian

PRAISE HIM WHO COMES!

(A Palm Sunday prayer)

Praise him who comes, and is to come! Hosanna to the Father's mighty Son, here and in the highest.

Praise him who once humbled himself in love to save our human race. Praise him for his Father's boundless grace!

Who would not stop to see and wonder at how low your love bent down? A donkey once carried you, here on the earth. You, in your might and holiness! And in your pity for us, you serve and bless our fallen race.

This day is joy-filled for all creation. My glad soul will sing a song of praise, and wave branches of thanksgiving that were once just palm branches, thrown in front of you by children.

Now we own your hidden majesty, and we cry with those children:

Hosanna to the Son of David!

Amen.

— Ephraim the Syrian

WE GO FORTH WITH PALM BRANCHES
TO MEET YOU *(A Palm Sunday prayer)*

You call us to a day of gladness, the one who came to us—
the King's own Son.

We go forth with palm branches to meet you, and angels
join us with trumpets as we shout loud hosannas.

All nations unite in one joy! Hosanna sounds in every tongue!

Loud praises rise to you, O Lord, from every creature.

The heavens in their quiet beauty praise your majesty. The
heights rejoice. The depths spring up to welcome you. The
sea and the land exult to feel your footsteps.

We bring you thanks, Lord, because you dwell among us.

Today the sun shines ten times brighter and rejoices with
glad radiance, paying tribute to the sun of glory who
brings light to all nations.

The moon does its best to spread luster and light over all
the heavens with its softest glow, adoring the one who
stooped so low for our sakes.

And all the stars of heaven dress in their finest festive
robes, bringing their celebration hymns as offerings to you
who have made them in all their beauty.

Today the forests rejoice. Each tree sings its own sweet anthem, because we wave their leafy branches as banners for the King of kings.

Let all of creation rejoice; we are no longer silent. The Heavenly One has come to us, sitting humbly on a foal. Let every village, every city, praise his name with a happy shout. Even the lips of infants are singing:

Blessed are you, the King who came!

Amen.

— *Ephraim the Syrian*

THE EARTH CELEBRATES YOUR VICTORY

(An Easter prayer)

Lord, the bright stars show their joy, while the earth pours forth its spring gifts.

Soft beds of violets paint the purple plain. The meadows are green with plants. Flowers come forth, while the herbs smile with their blossoms.

Corn springs up in the fields, promising to overcome our hunger. Trees renew their leafy shelter: mingled together, willow, fir, hazel, elm, maple, walnut … each tree applauds, delightful with its leaves.

The bee, humming over the flowers, carries off honey. The bird, once sluggish with the wintry cold, now returns to its song. The air sweetens with the melody.

The favor of the reviving world bears witness that all gifts have returned together with our Lord. For in honor of how you rose triumphant after your descent to the gloomy place of death, trees and flowers on every side show approval with leaves and flowers.

The light, the heavens, the fields, and the sea praise you, Lord. You crushed the laws of hell. You who were crucified reign as God over all things, and all created objects offer prayer to their creator.

We greet this festive day, to be reverenced throughout the world, the day you conquered hell, and gained the stars!

We applaud the changes of the months, the brightening light of days, the splendor of the hours. With their leaves the trees applaud in your honor. The vine, with its silent shoot, gives thanks. The thickets resound with the whisper of birds, and the sparrow sings with exuberant love. Amen.

— *Lactantius*

Notes

1   Irenaeus of Lyons, "Irenæus against Heresies," in *The Apostolic Fathers with Justin Martyr and Irenaeus*, ed. Alexander Roberts, James Donaldson, and A. Cleveland Coxe, Ante-Nicene Fathers 1 (Buffalo: Christian Literature Company, 1885), 3.6.4.

2   Jerome, "The Dialogue against the Luciferians," in Nicene and Post-Nicene Fathers 2.6, ed. Philip Schaff and Henry Wace (Buffalo: Christian Literature Publishing Co., 1893).

Biographies and Sources

Adæus and Maris

Known as "Teachers of the Easterns," tradition holds that Adæus and Maris composed an early order of worship around the year AD 200. It is still used today by Christians in Kurdistan.

Adæus is said to have originally served as a missionary in Mesopotamia, Syria, and Persia. His preaching was instrumental in the conversion of Maris of Persia, who came to Christ, became the disciple of Adæus, and gave his fortune to the poor.

During the persecutions of Aurelian, Maris was martyred along with his family at Saint Ninfa, just outside of Rome.

Sources Quoted

> *The Fathers of the Third and Fourth Centuries: Lactantius, Venantius, Asterius, Victorinus, Dionysius, Apostolic Teaching and Constitutions, Homily, and Liturgies,* edited by Alexander Roberts, James Donaldson, and A. Cleveland Coxe, Ante-Nicene Fathers 7 (Buffalo: The Christian Literature Co., 1886).

Ambrose of Milan

Ambrose (Aurelius Ambrosius, c. 340–397) was one of the most influential church leaders of the fourth century. It's difficult to sort fact from fiction about his early life, but he was obviously born into an influential, aristocratic Roman family. His father seems to have died when Ambrose was about 15, and the family moved to Rome. There Ambrose studied law, literature, and rhetoric and graduated to hold public office.

He was governor of Aemilia-Liguria in northern Italy until 374, when he was suddenly drafted as bishop of Milan.

At first he resisted the offer—even hiding in a friend's house—since he wasn't trained in theology, or even baptized. But within a week he was baptized, and he stepped into his new role. Or perhaps he grew into it.

On the plus side, Ambrose was immediately popular, and already well-known as a political figure. He donated much of his wealth to charity, studied theology (he already knew Greek), and came to defend orthodox Christian positions against heresies.

Ambrose was able to effectively deal with politicians as well as the everyday needs of his congregations. He answered letters personally and valued unity in the church. Today his body may still be seen in the church of Saint Ambrogio in Milan.

Sources Quoted

> *Ambrose: Select Works and Letters*, edited by Philip Schaff and Henry Wace, Nicene and Post-Nicene Fathers 2.10 (New York: The Christian Literature Co., 1896).

> "Deus Creator Omnium" [Creator of the Earth and Sky], translated by Charles Bigg in *The English Hymnal* (London: Oxford University Press, 1906).

ANATOLIUS OF CONSTANTINOPLE

Anatolius, a priest from Alexandria, Egypt, may not have written as much as others—but what he did write was spirited and lively. Several of his hymns are still well-loved today, especially in the Greek islands. Anatolius is credited for breaking the poetic mold of the time, venturing off in new creative directions to write his own style of "harmonious prose." Perhaps this independent streak helped him stand for biblical orthodoxy while political pressures and power plays boiled during the time of the Council of Chalcedon in 451. Anatolius was bishop of Constantinople when that council met to reaffirm the divine and human natures of Christ against heresies that had sprung up over the years. Though we don't know exactly when Anatolius was born, we do know that he died in 458.

Sources Quoted

Hymns and Poetry of the Eastern Church, edited by Bernard Pick (New York: Eaton & Mains, 1908).

Hymns of the Eastern Church, edited by J. M. Neale (London: J. T. Hayes, 1866).

THE APOSTOLIC CONSTITUTIONS

The Apostolic Constitutions (sometimes called Constitutions of the Holy Apostles) are comprised of eight books, covering various aspects of church organization, worship, and a code of conduct. As a whole the constitutions are designed primarily for clergy, but they have also served as helpful guidelines for laity. And although they were traditionally credited to Clement of Rome, perhaps in an attempt to lend more gravity to their content, the books are almost certainly written by someone else—or perhaps by several authors. It's impossible to tell. Even so, these volumes are usually dated to around AD 375 or 380, and include valuable historical insight into how the early church was growing and changing. The sections containing an order of worship include many useful prayers.

Sources Quoted

> *The Fathers of the Third and Fourth Centuries: Lactantius,*
> *Venantius, Asterius, Victorinus, Dionysius, Apostolic*
> *Teaching and Constitutions, Homily, and Liturgies,*
> edited by Alexander Roberts, James Donaldson, and
> A. Cleveland Coxe, Ante-Nicene Fathers 7 (Buffalo:
> The Christian Literature Co., 1886).

> *The Twelve Patriarchs, Excerpts and Epistles, The*
> *Clementina, Apocrypha, Decretals, Memoirs of Edessa and*
> *Syraic Documents, Remains of the First* Ages, edited by
> Alexander Roberts, James Donaldson, and A. Cleveland
> Coxe, Ante-Nicene Fathers 8 (Buffalo: The Christian
> Literature Co., 1886).

ARNOBIUS

Arnobius (died c. 330) already enjoyed a successful career
as a public speaker in North Africa when he came to Christ,
possibly as the result of a dream. Though we know little
of his actual life, we do know he became an enthusiastic
advocate for the Christian faith, writing a seven-book
apologetic series called Adversus Gentes.

Arnobius was a strong proponent of Christian
monotheism and of Christ's divinity. He was also the first
to introduce the argument later known as Pascal's Wager—
that if a person cannot decide between two opposing views,
why not adhere to the one with the greatest advantages, or
fewest disadvantages? In other words, compared to the
alternative, what could be the downside of following the
God who offered forgiveness, joy, and eternal life?

Sources Quoted

> *The Fathers of the Third Century: Gregory Thaumaturgus, Dionysius the Great, Julius Africanus, Anatolius and Minor Writers, Methodius, Arnobius,* edited by Alexander Roberts, James Donaldson, and A. Cleveland Coxe, Ante-Nicene Fathers 6 (Buffalo: The Christian Literature Co., 1886).

ATHENOGENES

Little is known of this martyr, though he was briefly mentioned in the writings of Basil the Great, and he may have died around the year AD 305. Traditional accounts hold that he approached his death singing this Trinitarian hymn, called "Phos Hilaron," which would make it the earliest known complete Christian hymn outside of anything recorded in Scripture. He is reported to have left a written version with his disciples. Also known as the "Lamplighting Hymn," it was included in the Apostolic Constitutions in the late third or early fourth century, and was sung as a candle was lit from the lamp burning above the traditional tomb of Christ in Jerusalem. John Keble, a leader of the Oxford Movement within the Anglican Church, translated the original Greek into English meter in 1834. It is still in use today in a number of Christian traditions.

Sources Quoted

> John Keble, *The Christian Year, Lyra Innocentium and Other Poems* (London: Oxford University Press, 1914), 441.

> John Keble, "Hail Gladdening Light," in *Hymns Ancient and Modern* (London: William Clowes & Sons, 1868).

AUGUSTINE OF HIPPO

Aurelius Augustinus (354–430) was one of the most prolific Christian thinkers and writers of his time, playing an influential role in early church history. He was born in what is now Algeria, some forty miles from the Mediterranean coast. His respectable parents made sure he received an excellent education, even borrowing funds to do so, and he began his career teaching rhetoric in Carthage.

Ever restless in his twenties and brimming with ambition, Augustine soon left North Africa to make his mark in Rome and then Milan. But after teaching for only a few years, he turned to Jesus Christ and was baptized by Ambrose in 387; shortly afterward, he left Milan to return to North Africa.

Augustine was appointed presbyter (a position similar to a priest) in 391, and bishop of Hippo several years later. And he would write, battling schisms and heresies with his uniquely popular style. Even during his lifetime, his books were widely circulated throughout the Roman world.

He left behind a massive and carefully catalogued collection of writings (more than five million words!). They would prove popular in their day, but even more so for centuries to come. His two most influential works, *Confessions* (AD 400) and *The City of God* (AD 413 to 426) shaped the way we view Scripture and helped define much of Christian thought.

This extended collection of his prayers reflects much of his heart for God and his lifelong quest for holiness. As he once wrote, "Our heart is restless until it finds its place of rest in you."

Sources Quoted

> *The Confessions of Saint Augustine,* translated by E. B.
> Pusey (London: J. G. and F. Rivington, 1838).

> *King Alfred's Old English Version of St. Augustine's*
> *Soliloquies,* edited by Henry Lee Hargrove (New York:
> Henry Holt and Company, 1904).

> *St. Augustine: Expositions on the Book of Psalms,* edited by
> Philip Schaff, Nicene and Post-Nicene Fathers 1.8 (New
> York: The Christian Literature Co., 1887).

> *St. Augustine: On the Holy Trinity, Doctrinal Treatises,*
> *Moral Treatises,* edited by Philip Schaff, Nicene and Post-
> Nicene Fathers 1.3 (New York: The Christian Literature
> Co., 1887).

> *St. Augustine: Homilies on the Gospel of John, Homilies*
> *on the First Epistle of John, Soliloquies,* edited by Philip
> Schaff, Nicene and Post-Nicene Fathers 1.7 (New York:
> The Christian Literature Co., 1888).

AUSONIUS

Through his writings, Decimus Magnus Ausonius (c. 310–
395) offers us an inside look at the last days of the Roman
Empire, as well as a feel for his approach to living and
working as a professing lay Christian in a secular society.

We have no written evidence of when he accepted the
teachings of what had by then become the established
religion of the empire. (Emperor Constantine converted
in the year 312.) Some scholars even question his spiritual
sincerity, despite the pious language and spiritual depth of
his prayers. Who is to judge?

In any case, Ausonius began his career in Bordeaux as a humble teacher, but eventually became a respected scholar, poet, and travel writer, and even a tutor to the emperor's family. That connection seems to have served him well; he finished his career as a highly placed consul in the Roman government. More than 300 pages of his work survive to this day, including the prayers recorded here.

Sources Quoted

> *Ausonius*, translated by Hugh G. Evelyn White (London: William Heinemann; New York: G. P. Putnam's Sons, 1919).

BASIL OF CAESAREA

Also known as Basil the Great (330–379). Basil was a bishop in Caesarea Mazaca in Cappadocia, what is modern-day Turkey. He was known not only as a theologian who strongly supported the Nicene Creed, but also as a humanitarian who cared for the poor and underprivileged.

Basil, his brother Gregory of Nyssa, and his friend Gregory of Nazianzus together were known as the Cappadocian Fathers. His grandfather was a Christian martyr.

Though Basil was himself talented and well educated, his life changed drastically when he met the charismatic Bishop Eustathius of Sebaste. In a letter, Basil wrote that "Suddenly, I awoke as out of a deep sleep. I beheld the wonderful light of the Gospel truth, and I recognized the nothingness of the wisdom of the princes of this world" (Basil, Letter 223, 2, "Against Eustathius of Sebasteia," in NPNF 2.8).

As a theologian, preacher, and bishop, Basil had a considerable influence on church practice for centuries after his death. Many prayers attributed to him are included in church liturgies, though it's impossible to know with certainty if he actually penned all the words.

Basil is also known for strongly opposing the Arian heresy, which claimed that Jesus was himself created in time, and not co-eternal with God the Father. And he was at one point interested in the lives of solitary desert monks, but eventually found more common ground with communal Christian groups.

Even though penned throughout the troubled times during which he lived, Basil's writings are known for their optimism, tenderness, and even playfulness. His *De spiritu sancto* was an important early work on the doctrine of the Holy Spirit.

Sources Quoted

Basil: Letters and Select Works, edited by Philip Schaff and Henry Wace, Nicene and Post-Nicene Fathers 2.8 (New York: The Christian Literature Co., 1895).

JOHN CASSIAN

Born into a pious, well-to-do family around the year 360, John Cassian left his family's wealth behind to enter a seminary in Bethlehem with his friend Germanus. He spent several years in study there before stepping out with Germanus to visit isolated believers in Egypt.

The two were fascinated and impressed by the enduring faith of the saints they encountered there, and they spent countless hours talking and praying with them. The brief visit to those scattered prayer communities turned into an extended pilgrimage and, after seven years in the desert, the two friends finally returned to their original assignment in Bethlehem.

The adventures weren't over, however, and Cassian felt compelled once again to share life with those isolated prayer warriors in the desert. He soon returned to Africa, this time staying with believers in Libya. At the time, between AD 380 and 400, hundreds of monks had scattered across the North African desert, living isolated lives of prayer.

Civilization called him back a second time, and eventually Cassian was ordained as a deacon by John Chrysostom. By way of Rome, he made his way back to his birthplace of Gaul (today's France) where he helped establish Christian prayer communities in and around Marseilles. He put to use much of what had inspired him throughout his time with the desert monks.

In his later years, between 426 and 428, Cassian wrote three of his best-known works—*The Institutes, Conferences,* and *On the Incarnation.* He also faced head-on two of the most significant heresies of that time—Nestorianism (that Jesus was two separate and distinct persons) and Pelagianism (that Adam's sin only affected Adam). Cassian died shortly after the year 430.

Sources Quoted

"The Institutes of the Coenobia," in *Sulpitius Severus, Vincent of Lerins, John Cassian,* edited by Philip Schaff and Henry Wace, Nicene and Post-Nicene Fathers 2.11 (New York: The Christian Literature Co., 1894).

"On the Incarnation of the Lord, Against Nestorius," in *Sulpitius Severus, Vincent of Lerins, John Cassian,* edited by Philip Schaff and Henry Wace, Nicene and Post-Nicene Fathers 2.11 (New York: The Christian Literature Co., 1894).

John Chrysostom

Chrysostom, who was known by his first name (John) by those who knew him, was considered one of the church's finest speakers of his time. He must have been a great preacher; in Greek, Chrysostom means "Golden Mouth." He was born in Antioch around 345 or 347, studied rhetoric and theology, and soon became a deacon and presbyter (priest) in the largest church of that city. In straightforward, practical sermons, he was known for speaking against the abuse of authority both in the church and in politics, and he championed the cause of the poor. No doubt this caused him some trouble. When he was appointed archbishop of Constantinople in 397, he refused to host lavish parties—a stand which was more appreciated by his parishioners than by the wealthy. In his sermons and writings, he often warned against the dangers and evils of materialism, which seems especially relevant to us today. He also helped to found several hospitals, and was one of the most prolific authors of the early church—exceeded only by Origen and Augustine. John Chrysostom died in the year 407.

Sources Quoted

"Homily 24 on Matthew," in *St. Chrysostom: Homilies on the Gospel of Saint Matthew*, edited by Philip Schaff, Nicene and Post-Nicene Fathers 1.10 (New York: The Christian Literature Co., 1888).

St. Chrysostom: On the Priesthood, Ascetic Treatises, Select Homilies and Letters, Homilies on the Statues, edited by Philip Schaff, Nicene and Post-Nicene Fathers 1.9 (New York: The Christian Literature Co., 1889).

CLEMENT OF ALEXANDRIA

Clement of Alexandria (Titus Flavius Clemens, 150–215) was one of the best-known Christian apologists and thinkers in the Greek-speaking world of his day.

He was probably born in Athens, and thoroughly trained in Greek literature and philosophy, but that learning wasn't enough for him; he turned to Christ as an adult. Finding his way to the influential city of Alexandria, Egypt, he studied under Pantaenus, the leader of the Christian academy there. He became his teacher's assistant and around the year 190 succeeded Pantaenus as leader.

Over his lifetime, Clement was able to bring together Greek philosophy and Old Testament tradition, and was widely known for his ministry to the intellectuals of the day. His "Prayer to the Teacher," as well as his larger work, *The Instructor*, reflect his academic background.

"Let us remove the ignorance and darkness that spreads like a mist over our sight," he once wrote, "and let us get a vision of the true God." He died in Jerusalem.

Sources Quoted

"Exhortation to the Heathen," chapter 11, in *Fathers of the Second Century: Hermas, Tatian, Athenagoras, Theophilus, and Clement of Alexandria (Entire)*, edited by Alexander Roberts, James Donaldson, and A. Cleveland Coxe, Ante-Nicene Fathers 2 (Buffalo: The Christian Literature Co., 1885).

"The Instructor (Paedagogus)," books 1, 3, in *Fathers of the Second Century: Hermas, Tatian, Athenagoras, Theophilus, and Clement of Alexandria (Entire)*, edited by Alexander Roberts, James Donaldson, and A. Cleveland

Coxe, Ante-Nicene Fathers 2 (Buffalo: The Christian Literature Co., 1885).

"The Stromata," book 4, in *Fathers of the Second Century: Hermas, Tatian, Athenagoras, Theophilus, and Clement of Alexandria (Entire)*, edited by Alexander Roberts, James Donaldson, and A. Cleveland Coxe, Ante-Nicene Fathers 2 (Buffalo: The Christian Literature Co., 1885).

CLEMENT OF ROME

Though we know few accurate details of his life, Clement (Clemens Romanus) was clearly a leading figure in the earliest church, perhaps discipled and chosen for leadership by the apostle Peter himself. Clement's letter to the Corinthians (1 Clement) is widely considered genuine, and is one of the oldest known Christian documents outside of Scripture. The first of his prayers ("You Alone...") is taken from that letter.

Clement may also be the same person mentioned by the apostle Paul in Philippians 4:3, though the connection is unprovable. And although scholars disagree, Clement was also traditionally credited with authorship of a number of other works, including the Homilies and Apostolic Constitutions.

Clement is traditionally thought to have been born around the year 35 and martyred under Emperor Trajan by being tied to an anchor and thrown into the sea, around the year AD 101. He is often remembered with the image of the anchor—an anchor of faith.

Sources Quoted

Clementine Homilies and Apostolical Constitutions, Homily 3, edited by James Donaldson (Edinburgh: T&T Clark, 1870).

"The Epistle of St. Clement to the Corinthians," in *The Apostolic Fathers,* translated by J. B. Lightfoot (New York: Macmillan and Co., 1890).

"Syrian Clementine Liturgy," in *Ancient Collects and Other Prayers,* edited by William Bright (London: J. H. and Jas. Parker, 1864).

CYRIL OF JERUSALEM

Little is known of the early life of Cyril (315–386) until he became the bishop of Jerusalem. We do know that he was well-known for writing a series of 23 lectures to young believers, called "catechetical lectures." His messages were filled with references to God's love and forgiveness, which was somewhat unusual for his time. He had to put that view into practice in his own life after he was exiled from Jerusalem (repeatedly!) due to misunderstandings with political leaders.

Sources Quoted

"Catechetical Lecture 17," in *Cyril of Jerusalem, Gregory of Nazianzen,* edited by Philip Schaff and Henry Wace, Nicene and Post-Nicene Fathers 2.7 (New York: The Christian Literature Co., 1894).

The Didache

Other than the Bible itself, the anonymously written Didache is one of the earliest examples of practical teaching for the church, dealing mainly with instructions for baptism, Communion, and Christian ethics. Scholars date it from the first or possibly second century. This pastoral manual was apparently written in Greek from an early Jewish-Christian perspective, and is also known as The Lord's Teaching through the Twelve Apostles to the Nations. It includes the prayer here.

Sources Quoted

"The Lord's Teaching through the Twelve Apostles to the Nations," in *The Fathers of the Third and Fourth Centuries: Lactantius, Venantius, Asterius, Victorinus, Dionysius, Apostolic Teaching and Constitutions, Homily, and Liturgies,* edited by Alexander Roberts, James Donaldson, and A. Cleveland Coxe, Ante-Nicene Fathers 7 (Buffalo: The Christian Literature Co., 1886).

Ephraim the Syrian

Ephraim the Syrian (306–373) was known as a theologian and writer, but also as a prolific hymn writer and poet. Over 400 hymns penned by Ephraim still exist, not to mention what was undoubtedly lost. In each one, the poetry and musicality of the verse point to the Savior.

Ephraim was born in the Roman city of Nisibis, in what is today Turkey, and was discipled by James, the well-known bishop of Nisibis. While Ephraim's mentor is recorded as one who helped rally city defenses against unsuccessful Persian invasions in 338, 346, and 350, Ephraim would have been involved in encouraging the people of Nisibis during those times, as well.

Meanwhile, Ephraim was also busy ministering to people at a time when polytheism, Judaism, and early Christianity competed for the hearts and minds of Nisibis. For that reason, much of Ephraim's work advocated for biblical orthodoxy. And much of Ephraim's writing uses "shepherd" and (sheep) "fold" language. During challenging times, and despite disease, disaster, and invasion, Ephraim wanted his people to know the truth.

Ephraim died ministering to victims of a plague that had ravaged the region around Edessa, in southeast Turkey.

Sources Quoted

Hymns and Poetry of the Eastern Church, edited by Bernard Pick (New York: Eaton & Mains, 1908).

"Nineteen Hymns on the Nativity of Christ in the Flesh," hymn 2, from *The Early Church Fathers and Other Works,* translated by J. B. Morris (Edinburgh: Wm. B. Eerdmans, 1867).

"The Nisibene Hymns," translated by Sarsfield Stopford, in *Part 2: Gregory the Great, Ephraim Syrus, Aphrahat,* edited by Philip Schaff and Henry Wace, Nicene and Post-Nicene Fathers 2.13 (New York: The Christian Literature Co., 1898).

"Three Homilies," in *Part 2: Gregory the Great, Ephraim Syrus, Aphrahat,* edited by Philip Schaff and Henry Wace, Nicene and Post-Nicene Fathers 2.13 (New York: The Christian Literature Co., 1898).

EUSEBIUS

Eusebius of Caesarea served as bishop of Caesarea and was known as a theologian, apologist, and historian. He lived from around 260 until 340. He is sometimes known as Eusebius Pamphili, after his noted teacher Pamphilus.

As the "Father of Church History," Eusebius produced several important historical books, including a biography of Constantine the Great, the first Christian emperor. Though he has been criticized as being a cheerleader for the emperor, rather than a completely accurate historian, the work is still valuable.

His most important work, though, was a narrative history of the early church, from the time of the apostles up until his own time. In it, he mentions details about church leaders, controversies, and martyrs. Much of the account, however, is based on otherwise lost sources.

Sources Quoted

"The Oration of Constantine," in *Eusebius: Church History, Life of Constantine the Great, and Oration in Praise of Constantine*, edited by Philip Schaff and Henry Wace, Nicene and Post-Nicene Fathers 2.1 (New York: The Christian Literature Co., 1890).

GREGORY NAZIANZEN

Gregory was born around 325 (or as late as 329) in the town of Arianzus, in Asia Minor, and died in the same place in the year 389. He was one of three children, schooled at a famous academy in Caesarea (Cappadocia) and taught by Carterius—who may also have tutored John Chrysostom.

Gregory was a close friend of Basil, and together they had a large influence on Christian theology, an influence that continues to this day. He was especially effective in explaining and defending the concept of the Trinity, and is still sometimes known as "Gregory the Theologian."

Gregory emphasized in his preaching and writings the concept of Jesus being fully human, while fully God, in contrast to several heresies of the time. Though he was somewhat pressured into taking church leadership by his father (and by his friend Basil), he seemed to prefer a more contemplative life, and enjoyed writing poetry.

Sources Quoted

Hymns and Poetry of the Eastern Church, edited by Bernard Pick (New York: Eaton & Mains, 1908).

"Orations, Gregory Nazianzen," in *Cyril of Jerusalem, Gregory of Nazianzen,* edited by Philip Schaff and Henry Wace, Nicene and Post-Nicene Fathers 2.7 (New York: The Christian Literature Co., 1894).

GREGORY OF NYSSA

Gregory of Nyssa (335–395), along with his older brother Basil of Caesarea and their friend Gregory Nazianzen, are known as the Cappadocian Fathers. Though he was probably the quietest and least known of the three, he would contribute much toward the understanding of the Trinity among early believers, and toward the revised Nicene Creed in 381. Gregory was born into a large Christian family which experienced persecution, living in what is now Turkey. His grandfather was killed for his faith, and his parents had their property confiscated. He is also known today as an early opponent of slavery.

Sources Quoted

Gregory of Nyssa: Dogmatic Treatises, etc., edited by Philip Schaff and Henry Wace, Nicene and Post-Nicene Fathers 2.5 (New York: The Christian Literature Co., 1893).

Life of St. Macrina (Suffolk: Richard Clay & Sons, 1916).

HILARY OF POITIERS

Largely overshadowed by more well-known figures and overlooked by most church historians, Hilary of Poitiers was an outstanding Christian thinker of his time.

He was born into an upper-class family around the year 300 in Poitiers, a city on the Clain River in what is now west-central France. His work reflects that he was thoroughly educated in the best Roman tradition, bilingual in Greek and Latin. And though he was well trained in literature and philosophy, he was also versed in natural history. In much of his work and theological arguments he uses illustrations from the natural world, from fig trees to hissing vipers.

Hilary was eventually drawn to faith by a desire to discover truth. Much like C. S. Lewis, he came to faith in Christ through a personal study of the Scriptures. We're not certain of the year of his conversion, however, and we're also not certain of his occupation at the time, or even if he was married. But his great mind and his writings would be linked to two other noted theologians who would follow him—Ambrose and Augustine.

In about the year 350 Hilary became bishop of Poitiers. And although recorded details of his life are scarce, we do know that he met some difficulty on account of his outspokenness. He was called to account by church authorities and exiled to Asia Minor in 356. He defended biblical orthodoxy until his death in 367.

Sources Quoted

"On the Trinity," in *Hilary of Poitiers, John of Damascus,* edited by Philip Schaff and Henry Wace, Nicene and Post-Nicene Fathers 2.9 (New York: The Christian Literature Co., 1899).

IRENAEUS OF LYONS

Born around AD 130, Irenaeus grew up in Asia Minor and studied under Polycarp in Smyrna—who was recorded as a disciple of the apostle John and was greatly influenced by the teachings of Justin Martyr.

Irenaeus eventually made his way to Rome, and from there to Gaul (what is modern-day France). As a bishop in Lugdunum (today's Lyons), he aimed much of his teaching against heresies that had sprung up, and toward defending the faith. His concern for keeping the church from splintering helped shape Christianity of that day, and his influence has remained over the centuries.

Traditional accounts record that Irenaeus was martyred for his faith around the year 200.

Sources Quoted

"Fragments from the Lost Writings of Irenaeus," in *The Apostolic Fathers with Justin Martyr and Irenaeus,* edited by Alexander Roberts, James Donaldson, and A. Cleveland Coxe, Ante-Nicene Fathers 1 (Buffalo: The Christian Literature Co., 1885).

"Iraenaeus Against Heresies," in *The Apostolic Fathers with Justin Martyr and Irenaeus*, edited by Alexander Roberts and James Donaldson, Ante-Nicene Fathers 1 (Buffalo: The Christian Literature Co., 1885).

LACTANTIUS

Lactantius (ca. 250–325) is best known for his service as advisor to Roman Emperor Constantine, and is assumed to have had an influence on that emperor's emerging Christian policies. Lactantius was also tutor to the emperor's son Crispus.

He was also an influential writer, known for his apologetic works such as his *Divine Institutes*, or *Institutiones Divinae*. He presented the gospel message to pagan audiences in ways they could understand, and was particularly interested in end-times prophecy—though he believed the end times would be marked by the breakup of the Roman Empire.

Sources Quoted

The Fathers of the Third and Fourth Centuries: Lactantius, Venantius, Asterius, Victorinus, Dionysius, Apostolic Teaching and Constitutions, Homily, and Liturgies, edited by Alexander Roberts, James Donaldson, and A. Cleveland Coxe, Ante-Nicene Fathers 7 (Buffalo: The Christian Literature Co., 1886).

MELITO OF SARDIS

Melito, bishop of Sardis, served his church during the reign of Marcus Aurelius in the second century, and died around the year AD 180. Other than the high regard other church leaders expressed of him, we know little of his life's details. He is however perhaps best known for his influence in putting together the earliest Christian Old Testament canon. (His list, the first known example that we know of, did leave out the book of Esther.)

Melito was also a champion for the truth of Christ's divinity, holding that Jesus was both fully human and fully divine. And although he reportedly wrote many works, referred to by others, most of those works have not survived. This adapted prayer is a fragment of what remains, which was also quoted by Lactantius—the Christian advisor to Roman Emperor Constantine.

Sources Quoted

> *The Twelve Patriarchs, Excerpts and Epistles, the Clementina, Apocrypha, Decretals, Memoirs of Edessa and Syriac Documents, Remains of the First Ages*, edited by Alexander Roberts, James Donaldson, and A. Cleveland Coxe, Ante-Nicene Fathers 8 (Buffalo: The Christian Literature Co., 1886).

METHODIUS OF OLYMPIA

A bit of mystery surrounds the life and work of Methodius of Olympia, who died around the year 311, perhaps as a martyr (we're not sure) after serving as (perhaps) bishop of Olympia in (probably) Lycia, southern Turkey, and (maybe) also in the Mediterranean port city of Tyre. Writings from that era that quote or mention Methodius give conflicting information.

We also don't know when he was born, or where, or anything about his family. He didn't leave behind a bio, or mention any of his life details in his writings.

In any case, we do know that Methodius was a leading church figure of the time, obviously well-educated, and a prolific writer. He is also known for his recurring theological disagreements with another church father, Origen. What will our bodies be like at the resurrection? Or what will the physical world be like in eternity? Those were the kinds of theological issues upon which Methodius and Origen disagreed.

Still, both of them contributed greatly to the foundation of the early church, and Methodius is especially known for his love of Christ displayed in his one complete surviving manuscript, which concludes in a hymn he wrote on Jesus as the bridegroom of the church.

Sources Quoted

"On the Holy Theophany, or on Christ's Baptism," in *The Fathers of the Third Century: Gregory Thaumaturgus, Dinoysius the Great, Julius Africanus, Anatolius and Minor Writers, Methodius, Arnobius*, edited by Alexander Roberts, James Donaldson, and A. Cleveland Coxe, Ante-Nicene Fathers 6 (Buffalo: Christian Literature Co., 1886).

"Oration Concerning Simeon and Anna," in *The Fathers of the Third Century: Gregory Thaumaturgus, Dionysius the Great, Julius Africanus, Anatolius and Minor Writers, Methodius, Arnobius*, edited by Alexander Roberts, James Donaldson, and A. Cleveland Coxe, Ante-Nicene Fathers 6 (Buffalo: The Christian Literature Co., 1886).

Odes of Solomon

Since their recovery from a Syriac manuscript in 1909, the Odes of Solomon have been identified as a very early messianic Jewish book of praise, most likely used in Christian worship. The author is unknown, though it appears that the 41 separate verses could date from as early as AD 125— within a century of Christ's death and resurrection. They're called the Odes of Solomon not because they were actually written by Solomon, but because their form continues in the written tradition of the ancient Jewish king.

Sources Quoted

> J. Rendel Harris, *The Odes and Psalms of Solomon, Now First Published from the Syriac Version* (Cambridge: Cambridge University Press, 1909).

PAULINUS PELLAEUS

Paulinus (377–461) was born at Pella in central Macedonia (Greece) to a wealthy Roman family, and moved to Bordeaux when he was three. Sadly, however, the family lost nearly everything when his father died and Bordeaux was sacked by Visigoths in 414. They had no choice but to flee for their lives. When still more family members died, including his wife and two sons, Paulinus escaped to a small farm in Marseilles before eventually returning again to Bordeaux. Having experienced so much deep loss and sadness, he wrote the autobiographical poem *Eucharisticus* (which means "thanksgiving") in his final years, at age 83. It's an extended look back on how God worked in his life through invasions and deep loss and during the fall of the Roman Empire. The autobiography includes several poignant prayers, included here.

Sources Quoted

The Eucharisticus of Paulinus Pellaeus, in *Ausonius,*
translated by Hugh G. Evelyn White (London: William
Heinemann; New York: G. P. Putnam's Sons, 1921).

POLYCARP

Polycarp (69–155) was an early Christian martyr, church
leader, and disciple of the apostle John. He served as bishop
of Smyrna, and is significant for being one of the earliest
believers whose writings have survived. His epistle To the
Philippians is believed to have been written in the early
second century, and urges Christians to stand fast against
heresy.

Polycarp's career was also distinguished by the fact that
he had contact with, and was influenced by, many of the
original disciples of Jesus.

Polycarp's life ended violently during Roman persecution
when he refused to deny his Lord. When asked one last
time to disown his faith, he is reported to have said, "Eighty
and six years I have served him, and he has done me no
wrong. How can I speak evil of my king who saved me?"
His final prayer before being burned at the stake, included
here, was recorded by the historian Eusebius.

Sources Quoted

The Apostolic Fathers with Justin Martyr and Irenaeus, ed.
Alexander Roberts, James Donaldson, and A. Cleveland
Coxe, Ante-Nicene Fathers 1 (Buffalo: The Christian
Literature Company, 1885).

PSEUDO-MACARIUS

A few generations after his death, a book called *Fifty Spiritual Homilies* appeared in the name of Macarius of Egypt (300–391). While these homilies by an anonymous author are now known to have not been written by Macarius of Egypt, they had a long-lasting influence on Eastern monasticism and Protestant pietism.

Sources Quoted

Fifty Spiritual Homilies of St. Macarius the Egyptian, edited by A. J. Mason (London: Society for Promoting Christian Knowledge; New York: Macmillan, 1921).

SERAPION SCHOLASTICUS

Serapion (d. 370) served as a bishop of Thmuis (or Tell el-Timai, near the modern city of El-Mansoura) in Egypt's Nile delta region. A former monk, he played a key role in the early struggles against heresy—particularly Arianism, which claimed that God the Father had created Jesus at some point. His orthodox positions put him at odds for a time with Emperor Constantius II, even to the point of banishment. Still, Serapion was considered a brilliant scholar. He is remembered for compiling the *Euchologion of Serapion*—a sort of prayer handbook, or sacramentary, for worship leaders. The prayers included here were part of that work.

Sources Quoted

Bishop Sarapion's Prayer-Book: An Egyptian Pontifical Dated Probably about A.D. 350–56, edited by John Wordsworth, translated by G. Wobbermin (London: Society for Promoting Christian Knowledge, 1899).

SYNESIUS

Synesius (c. 375 to 413) was born in Cyrene, an ancient Greek city on the North African coast. As a student of Hypatia, the female philosopher, he became known more as a philosopher and poet himself, though he somewhat reluctantly served as bishop of Ptolemais, on the Mediterranean coast. His career there was marked with political upheavals and personal tragedies (his three sons died toward the end of his life), but he maintained a lively interest in a variety of subjects, including philosophy and science. Despite his creative reputation, little of his poetry and hymns have survived.

Sources Quoted

Hymns and Poetry of the Eastern Church, edited by Bernard Pick (New York: Eaton & Mains, 1908).

SHAMUNA THE MARTYR

During the days of persecution, Rome often found their ultimate victims in the early Christian church. This prayer is passed along to us by Simeon Metaphrastes, an eleventh-century saint and historian, about one such incident. It details the execution of Shamuna, a believer from Edessa—what is today Turkey—who refused to deny Christ and sacrifice to the Roman gods. It mentions that "Thus did he utter the praise of the Umpire of the strife, and a scribe who was present took down in writing what was said." The persecution is said to have taken place in the ninth year of Diocletian's reign, which would have placed it around AD 293.

Sources Quoted

Simeon Metaphrastes, "Martyrdom of the Holy Confessors Shamuna, Guria, and Habib," in *The Twelve Patriarchs, Excerpts and Epistles, The Clementina, Apocrypha, Decretals, Memoirs of Edessa and Syriac Documents, Remains of the First Ages*, edited by Alexander Roberts, James Donaldson, and A. Cleveland Coxe, Ante-Nicene Fathers 8 (Buffalo: The Christian Literature Co., 1886).

TERTULLIAN

Tertullian (c. 155–220) played an important role in developing early Christian thought and theology. From his home in Carthage (in the Roman province of North Africa) Quintus Septimius Florens Tertullianus wrote what would become a sizable library of Christian literature, with an emphasis on apologetics and including several works against heresy. He was the first writer in Latin to use the term "Trinity" (in Latin, "trinitas"), and was called the "father of Latin Christianity" as well as the "founder of Western theology."

Though we're not certain, Tertullian may have been a lawyer earlier in life. Through his prolific writings, he was a literary mentor to another important early church leader, Cyprian of Carthage, and laid a theological framework for Augustine, who would be born in the same area some 135 years later.

The prayer included here is from his book *On Repentance*.

Sources Quoted

"On Repentance," in *Latin Christianity: Its Founder,
Tertullian, I. Apologetic; II. Anti-Marcion; III. Ethical,*
edited by Alexander Roberts, James Donaldson, and
A. Cleveland Coxe, Ante-Nicene Fathers 3 (Buffalo:
The Christian Literature Co., 1885).

THEODORET

His name means "Given by God," and Theodoret's well-
to-do, aristocratic parents certainly felt it was appropriate
after long years of not being able to have children. Born in
AD 393, Theodoret, or Theodoretus, lived up to his name as
he studied Greek, Syriac, and Hebrew, preparing for service
in the church. In fact, after his parents died he gave away his
inheritance and lived a life of poverty. He became a priest on
the Mediterranean island of Cyprus and dedicated his life to
serving God and the people around him. He had a heart for
evangelism and was well known for his fervent preaching.
And like many other early church leaders, he was seriously
challenged when he stood up for biblical truth in opposition
to heresy. Theodoret died around the year 458.

Sources Quoted

"Letters of the Blessed Theodoret, Bishop of Cyprus," in
Theodoret, Jerome, Gennadius, Rufinus: Historical Writings,
etc., edited by Philip Schaff and Henry Wace, Nicene
and Post-Nicene Fathers 2.3 (New York: The Christian
Literature Co., 1892).

VENANTIUS

Italian church leader and poet Venantius Honorius
Clementianus Fortunatus was born near Treviso, Italy,
around the year 530, attended school at Ravenna and Milan,
and came to know Christ at an early age. After being healed
of an eye disease (some accounts include miraculous
details), he traveled to France, where he wrote love songs
and eventually joined the Abbey of St. Croix in Poitiers. He
became its bishop in 599. Much of the music he composed
is today lost, though a few of his hymns dealing with the
cross of Christ survive. He died in 609.

Sources Quoted

"Poem of Venantius Honorius Clementianus Fortunatus,
On Easter," in *The Fathers of the Third and Fourth
Centuries: Lactantius, Venantius, Asterius, Victorinus,
Dionysius, Apostolic Teaching and Constitutions, Homily,
and Liturgies,* edited by Alexander Roberts, James
Donaldson, and A. Cleveland Coxe, Ante-Nicene
Fathers 7 (Buffalo: The Christian Literature Co., 1886).

INDEX OF AUTHORS

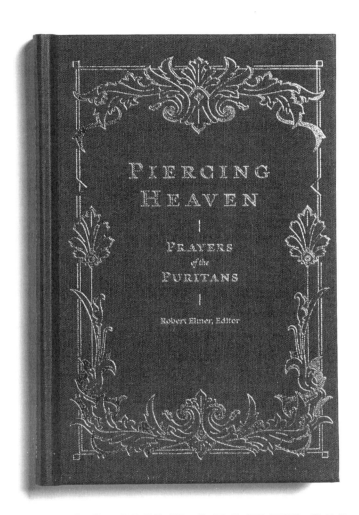

ALSO AVAILABLE FROM LEXHAM PRESS

Piercing Heaven: Prayers of the Puritans

—

**Visit lexhampress.com
to learn more**